TABLE OF CONTENT

Introduction	2
Chapter 1: Breezy Breakfasts	6
Chapter 2: Cool Soups and Sandwiches	19
Chapter 3: Sunsational Salads and Sides	38
Chapter 4: Fresh from the Sea	63
Chapter 5: Easy Summer Poultry	86
Chapter 6: Burgers, Dogs, and Other Meat Dishes	101
Chapter 7: Vegetarian's Paradise	117

INTRODUCTION
SOUTH BEACH DIET FOR THE SUMMER

Summer is a great time to enjoy your South Beach Diet lifestyle. With the abundance of fresh fruits and vegetables available at this time of year, it's so easy to eat healthy. Whether you shop at a local farmers' market or supermarket or enjoy the bounty of your own garden, the foods of summer naturally suit the South Beach Diet.

Since we all like to relax during these warm months, preparing food should be laid-back and fun. The easy recipes in this book help you do just that, any night of the week, whether you're eating in or making food for a picnic, barbecue, camping trip, day at the beach, or ballgame. Imagine packing a cooler with South Beach Diet Club Sandwiches, a side of Savoy Slaw with Sesame Dressing, and fresh Summer Fruit Cocktail for dessert. Add some plastic utensils, a few napkins, and a bottle of water and you're good to go! Burgers, hot dogs, fries, and creamy potato and egg salads are on everyone's list of summer favorites, including ours, so we've updated them —creating healthy versions that are tastier than ever. Juicy Chimichurri Burgers are made with lean ground beef, and there are Asian Tuna Burgers and South-of-the-Border Salmon Burgers, too. We've lightened up potato salad with a creamy yogurt dressing and egg salad by using more egg whites than yolks. Hot dogs are dressed with a homemade tomato and pickle relish that's sugar free and much lower in sodium than supermarket versions. For vegetarians, there are tasty Chicago-style tofu dogs, charred on the grill and topped with hot peppers, ripe tomato slices, tangy mustard, and more. You'll make delicious grilled fries using fiber-rich sweet potatoes, and refreshing Peach-Raspberry Shakes that taste as rich as those made with ice cream. And this is just the beginning!

By thinking ahead and doing some advance preparation, you can save valuable time to relax and enjoy more summer fun.

The Phases: A Short Course

Here are the fundamentals of the South Beach Diet's 3 phases:

Phase 1: This is the shortest phase of the diet, lasting only 2 weeks. Phase 1 is for people who have a substantial amount of weight to lose or who experience significant cravings for sugar and refined starches. During this phase, you'll jump-start your weight loss and stabilize your blood sugar levels to minimize cravings by eating a diet rich in healthy lean protein (fish, chicken, and lean cuts of beef), vegetables, nuts, reduced-fat cheeses, eggs, low-fat dairy, and good unsaturated fats, such as extra-virgin olive oil. You'll enjoy three satisfying meals a day, plus at least two snacks, and you'll even be able to have some desserts. What you won't be eating are starches (bread, pasta, and rice) or sugar (including fruit and fruit juices). While this may be hard at first, remember that in just 2 weeks you'll be adding many of these foods back into your life. Exercise during all phases is important to your overall health and will improve your results.

Phase 2: Those people who have 10 pounds or less to lose, who don't have problems with cravings, or who simply want to improve their health can start the diet with Phase 2. If you're moving on to Phase 2 from Phase 1, you'll find that your weight will continue to drop steadily and your cravings will have subsided. You'll gradually reintroduce many of the foods that were off-limits on Phase 1, including more good carbs such as whole-grain breads, whole-wheat pasta, and brown rice, as well as whole fruits and some root vegetables (such as sweet potatoes). You'll even be able to have a glass or two of red or white wine with meals if you like. Continue on Phase 2 until you reach a weight that's healthy for you.

Phase 3: This phase begins once you reach your healthy weight. At this point, you'll fully understand how to make good food choices while maintaining your health and weight. Since your South Beach Diet lifestyle will be second nature and you'll be able to monitor your body's response to particular foods with ease, you'll find yourself naturally making the right choices. Remember, once you reach Phase 3, no food is off-limits. You can even enjoy a few bites of a decadent dessert on occasion.

CHAPTER 1
BREEZY BREAKFASTS

FARMER'S CHEESE PANCAKES WITH SUMMER FRUITS

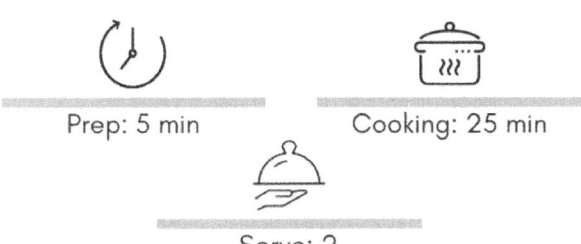

Prep: 5 min Cooking: 25 min Serve: 2

NUTRITION:
Per serving with fruit: 230 calories, 12 g fat, 5 g saturated fat, 19 g protein, 8 g carbohydrate, 1 g fiber, 340 mg sodium

INGREDIENTS

Topping
- 2 medium peaches, sliced (1 cup)
- 1/4 cup water
- 2 tablespoons granular sugar substitute
- 1 teaspoon fresh lemon juice
- 1/4 cup raspberries

Pancakes
- 6 large eggs, lightly beaten
- 1 cup semisoft farmer's cheese
- 2 teaspoons granular sugar substitute

DIRECTION

1. Heat the oven to 200°F.
2. For the topping: In a small saucepan, combine peaches, water, and sugar substitute; bring to a boil over medium heat. Reduce the heat to low and simmer until peaches are soft, about 10 minutes. Remove from the heat and stir in lemon juice. Gently stir in raspberries; set aside and keep warm.
3. While the topping is cooking, make the pancakes: In a large bowl, whisk together eggs, 1/3 cup of the cheese, and sugar substitute.
4. Lightly coat an 8-inch nonstick skillet with cooking spray and heat over medium heat. Spoon 1/4 cup of the batter into the pan and cook until pancake is set and edges are starting to turn golden, about 2 minutes. Loosen with a rubber spatula and flip; cook 1 minute more. Transfer pancake to a heatproof platter and place in the oven to keep warm. Repeat for remaining pancakes.
5. Divide pancakes among 4 plates. Spoon peach-raspberry topping over pancakes and dollop with remaining cheese. Serve warm.

SUMMER SQUASH SCRAMBLE WITH FRESH TOMATO

Prep: 15 min   Cooking: 10 min   Serve: 2

NUTRITION:
Per serving: 180 calories, 12 g fat, 2.5 g saturated fat, 11 g protein, 8 g carbohydrate, 2 g fiber, 390 mg sodium

INGREDIENTS

- 3 large eggs
- 1 teaspoon chopped chives
- 1/4 teaspoon salt
- 1/8 teaspoon freshly ground black pepper
- 2 teaspoons canola oil
- 1 small yellow summer squash, halved and thinly sliced into half-moons
- 1/2 small onion, finely chopped
- 1 medium tomato, finely chopped

DIRECTION

1. In a small bowl, beat eggs, chives, salt, and pepper until well combined.
2. In a medium nonstick skillet, heat oil over medium heat. Add squash and onion; cook, stirring occasionally, until softened and starting to brown, about 8 minutes
3. Add egg mixture to the skillet and cook, stirring frequently, until eggs are set, about 2 minutes. Spoon eggs onto 2 plates and sprinkle with tomato. Serve warm.

SWEET STRAWBERRIES WITH GREEK-STYLE YOGURT AND ALMONDS

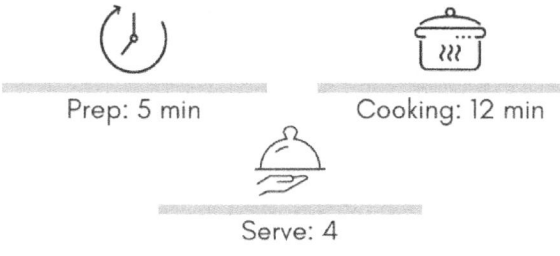

Prep: 5 min   Cooking: 12 min   Serve: 4

NUTRITION:
Per serving: 190 calories, 7 g fat, 0.5 g saturated fat, 11 g protein, 26 g carbohydrate, 4 g fiber, 105 mg sodium

INGREDIENTS

- 1/2 cup sliced almonds
- 3 cups nonfat or low-fat Greek-style plain yogurt
- 3 cups sliced strawberries

DIRECTION

1. Heat the oven to 275°F. Spread almonds on a baking sheet and bake until fragrant and lightly browned, 10 to 12 minutes.
2. Divide yogurt evenly among 4 bowls. Top each serving with 3/4 cup strawberries and 2 tablespoons almonds.

BLUEBERRY-ALMOND BRAN MUFFINS

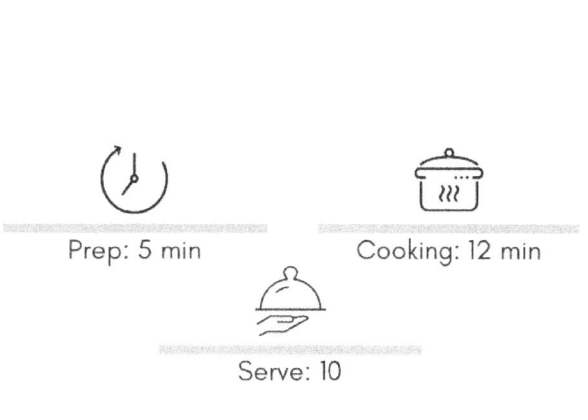

Prep: 5 min Cooking: 12 min Serve: 10

NUTRITION:
Per serving: 150 calories, 8 g fat, 1 g saturated fat, 5 g protein, 17 g carbohydrate, 5 g fiber, 200 mg sodium

INGREDIENTS

- 1 cup whole-grain pastry flour
- 1 cup wheat bran
- 1/2 cup all-purpose white flour
- 2 tablespoons granular sugar substitute
- 1+1/2 teaspoons ground cinnamon
- 1+1/4 teaspoons baking soda
- 1/4 teaspoon freshly ground nutmeg
- 1/4 teaspoon salt
- 1+1/4 cups 1% or fat-free buttermilk
- 2 large eggs, lightly beaten
- 1/4 cup canola oil
- 1+1/2 teaspoons vanilla extract
- 1+1/4 cups blueberries
- 1/3 cup sliced almonds

DIRECTION

1. Heat the oven to 350°F. Lightly coat a 12-cup muffin tin with cooking spray.
2. In a large bowl, combine pastry flour, bran, white flour, sugar substitute, cinnamon, baking soda, nutmeg, and salt.
3. In a medium bowl, whisk together buttermilk, eggs, oil, and vanilla. Make a well in the center of the dry ingredients. Add wet ingredients to dry and mix just to combine; do not overmix.
4. Gently fold blueberries into batter. Divide batter evenly among muffin cups. Top with almonds and gently press them into batter. Bake muffins for 25 minutes, or until a tester inserted in the center comes out clean. Cool in the pan for 5 minutes and then remove to a rack to finish cooling.

EASY WALNUT MUESLI WITH FRESH APRICOTS

Prep: 5 min Cooking: 12 min Serve: 8

NUTRITION:
Per serving: 264 calories, 15 g fat, 1.5 g saturated fat, 11 g protein, 25 g carbohydrate, 5 g fiber, 28 mg sodium

INGREDIENTS

Muesli
- 1 cup chopped walnuts
- 1+1/2 cups rolled oats
- 1/2 cup wheat germ
- 1/4 cup pumpkin seeds
- 1/4 cup sunflower seeds

Toppings
- 2 tablespoons ground flaxseed
- 8 fresh apricots, sliced (2 cups)
- 2 cups 1% or fat-free milk

DIRECTION

1. For the muesli: Heat the oven to 275°F. Spread walnuts on a baking sheet and bake until fragrant and lightly browned, about 12 minutes. In a large bowl, combine walnuts, oats, wheat germ, pumpkin seeds, and sunflower seeds.
2. For each serving, place 1/2 cup muesli in a cereal bowl. Top each with 3/4 teaspoon flaxseed and 1/4 cup apricots. Add 1/4 cup milk and serve.

GREET-THE-SUN BREAKFAST PIZZAS

Prep: 10 min Cooking: 20 min

Serve: 20

NUTRITION:
Per serving: 250 calories, 13 g fat, 3.5 g saturated fat, 13 g protein, 21 g carbohydrate, 3 g fiber, 500 mg sodium

INGREDIENTS

- 5 teaspoons extra-virgin olive oil
- 4 ounces packed spinach (4 cups)
- 2 (6-inch) whole-grain pitas, halved horizontally
- 2 large plum tomatoes, thinly sliced
- 4 large eggs
- 1/4 teaspoon salt
- 1/4 teaspoon freshly ground black pepper
- 2 ounces reduced-fat feta cheese, crumbled (1/3 cup)

DIRECTION

1. Heat the oven to 450°F.
2. In a large nonstick skillet, heat 1 teaspoon of the oil over medium heat. Add spinach, in batches if necessary, and cook until wilted, 2 to 3 minutes.
3. Brush inside of each pita round with 1 teaspoon oil. Place pita rounds, oiled side up, on a large baking sheet and bake until starting to brown, about 5 minutes. Remove from the oven.
4. Divide tomatoes and spinach evenly among pita halves, leaving an empty space in the center of each for an egg. Crack 1 egg into the center of each pita.
5. Sprinkle with salt and pepper, return to the oven, and bake until yolks are lightly set, 8 to 10 minutes. Sprinkle with cheese and continue baking until cheese has softened, about 2 minutes more. Serve warm.

SWEET POTATO AND TURKEY HASH

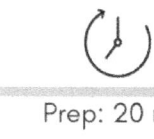
Prep: 20 min

Cooking: 12 min

Serve: 4

NUTRITION:
Per serving: 120 calories, 4.5 g fat, 1.5 g saturated fat, 12 g protein, 9 g carbohydrate, 2 g fiber, 190 mg sodium

INGREDIENTS

- 2 teaspoons extra-virgin olive oil
- 1 small (8-ounce) sweet potato, peeled and finely chopped
- 1 small red bell pepper, finely chopped
- 2 scallions, thinly sliced
- 2 tablespoons water
- 1/4 teaspoon salt
- 1/8 teaspoon freshly ground black pepper
- 1/8 teaspoon dried thyme
- 1/2 pound cooked skinless roast turkey breast, cut into 1/4-inch cubes (1 cup)
- 2 tablespoons reduced-fat sour cream

DIRECTION

1. In a large nonstick skillet, heat oil over medium heat. Add sweet potato and cook, stirring occasionally, until lightly browned and beginning to soften, about 5 minutes. Add bell pepper, scallions, water, salt, black pepper, and thyme; cook until bell pepper and scallions are softened, about 5 minutes.
2. Stir in turkey and cook until heated through, about 2 minutes. Remove from the heat and stir in sour cream. Serve warm.

WHOLE-GRAIN NECTARINE PANCAKES

Prep: 10 min | Cooking: 20 min
Serve: 4

NUTRITION:
Per serving: 290 calories, 15 g fat, 4.5 g saturated fat, 9 g protein, 30 g carbohydrate, 3 g fiber, 490 mg sodium

INGREDIENTS

- 1 cup whole-grain pastry flour
- 3 teaspoons granular sugar substitute
- 1 teaspoon baking soda
- 1 cup 1% or fat-free buttermilk
- 2 large eggs, lightly beaten
- 1/4 cup trans-fat-free margarine, melted, plus 1 tablespoon unmelted
- 1-2 medium nectarines, sliced (1 cup)
- 1/4 teaspoon ground cinnamon

DIRECTION

1. Heat the oven to 200°F.
2. In a large bowl, combine flour, 2 teaspoons of the sugar substitute, and baking soda.
3. In a medium bowl, whisk together buttermilk, eggs, and melted margarine. Make a well in the center of the dry ingredients. Add wet ingredients to dry and mix just to combine; do not overmix.
4. Coat a large nonstick skillet or griddle with cooking spray and heat over medium heat until hot enough to cause drops of water to scatter over the surface, about 3 minutes. Working in batches if necessary, spoon a heaping tablespoon of batter onto the griddle to form a 3-inch pancake (you will be making 16 pancakes). Cook pancakes until golden brown, about 2 minutes per side. Transfer to a heatproof platter and place in the oven to keep warm until ready to serve.
5. In a medium nonstick skillet, heat remaining 1 tablespoon margarine over medium heat until melted. Add nectarines, cinnamon, and remaining 1 teaspoon sugar substitute. Cook, stirring occasionally, until nectarines are soft and golden, about 5 minutes. Remove pancakes from the oven and divide among 4 plates. Spoon nectarine slices over pancakes and serve

BLACKBERRY -BANANA BREAKFAST SMOOTHIES

Prep: 10 min Cooking: 20 min Serve: 4

NUTRITION:
Per serving: 100 calories, 0.5 g fat, 0 g saturated fat, 5 g protein, 21 g carbohydrate, 3 g fiber, 50 mg sodium

INGREDIENTS

- 2 small bananas, quartered (1+1/2 cups)
- 1 cup blackberries, plus extra for garnish (optional)
- 1+1/2 cups nonfat or low-fat plain yogurt
- 1 tablespoon granular sugar substitute (optional)
- 1 tablespoon wheat germ
- 4 ice cubes

DIRECTION

1. In a blender, combine bananas and blackberries; purée until smooth. Add yogurt, sugar substitute, if using, wheat germ, and ice cubes; blend until smooth, about 1 minute. Pour into 4 (10-ounce) glasses, garnish with whole blackberries, if using, and serve.

POACHED EGGS WITH CHERRY TOMATOES AND SCALLIONS

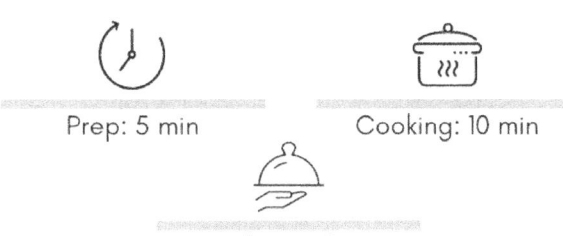

Prep: 5 min Cooking: 10 min

Serve: 2

NUTRITION:
Per serving: 160 calories, 12 g fat, 2.5 g saturated fat, 7 g protein, 7 g carbohydrate, 2 g fiber, 220 mg sodium

INGREDIENTS

- 1 tablespoon extra-virgin olive oil
- 2 scallions, thinly sliced
- 8 ounces cherry tomatoes, halved (1+1/4 cups)
- 1/8 teaspoon salt
- 2 teaspoons white vinegar
- 2 large eggs

DIRECTION

1. In a small nonstick skillet, heat oil over medium heat. Add scallions and cook until fragrant and beginning to soften, about 2 minutes. Add tomatoes and salt; cook, stirring occasionally, until tomatoes have softened and given off some of their juices, about 3 minutes. Remove the pan from the heat, cover, and keep warm.
2. Bring a large saucepan of water to a boil; add vinegar. Crack 1 egg into a cup. Gently slide egg into the water. Repeat with remaining egg, using a slotted spoon to keep eggs separated from each other, if necessary. Cook at a simmer until yolks are lightly set, 3 to 4 minutes.
3. Divide tomato-scallion mixture between 2 shallow bowls. Top each with an egg. Spoon any remaining liquid from the tomato mixture over the eggs. Serve warm.

THREE BERRY-STUFFED FRENCH TOAST

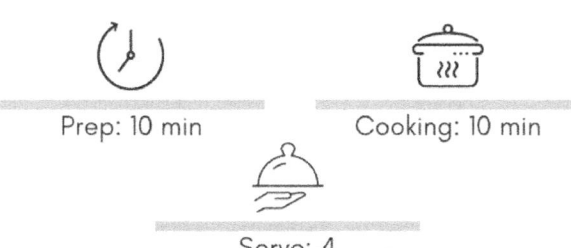

Prep: 10 min Cooking: 10 min Serve: 4

NUTRITION:
Per serving: 280 calories, 9 g fat, 3.5 g saturated fat, 17 g protein, 30 g carbohydrate, 5 g fiber, 470 mg sodium

INGREDIENTS

- 1/3 cup blackberries
- 1/3 cup blueberries
- 1/3 cup raspberries
- 2/3 cup semisoft farmer's cheese
- 1 tablespoon granular sugar substitute
- 8 slices whole-grain sandwich bread
- 3 large eggs
- 1/4 cup 1% milk
- 1/4 teaspoon ground cinnamon

DIRECTION

1. In a medium bowl, combine blackberries, blueberries, raspberries, cheese, and sugar substitute. Using a fork, mash together lightly. Lay 4 slices of the bread on a work surface.
2. Spread berry mixture evenly on slices and top with remaining bread slices to form 4 sandwiches. Lightly press around the edges to seal. In a shallow dish, beat eggs with milk and cinnamon. Dip both sides of sandwiches into egg mixture, allow excess to drip off, and place sandwiches on a platter.
3. Lightly coat a nonstick skillet or griddle with cooking spray and heat over medium heat. Cook French toast in two batches until golden brown, about 2 minutes per side. Serve warm.

SMOKED SALMON AND CREAM CHEESE "BREAKWICHES"

Prep: 10 min   Cooking: 10 min   Serve: 4

NUTRITION:
Per serving: 240 calories, 11 g fat, 4.5 g saturated fat, 19 g protein, 18 g carbohydrate, 5 g fiber, 810 mg sodium

INGREDIENTS

- 8 slices thin-sliced whole-grain bread
- 2 ounces reduced-fat cream cheese (1/4 cup)
- 6 ounces thinly sliced smoked salmon
- 2 tablespoons chopped chives
- Freshly ground black pepper
- 4 teaspoons trans-fat-free margarine

DIRECTION

1. Lay bread on a work surface; spread each slice with 1 tablespoon of the cream cheese. Divide smoked salmon among 4 of the slices. Sprinkle salmon evenly with chives and pepper. Top with remaining bread slices to make 4 sandwiches.
2. In a large nonstick skillet, heat 2 teaspoons of the margarine over medium heat. Add 2 sandwiches, weight down with a heavy pan, and cook until golden brown, about 2 minutes per side. Repeat with remaining margarine and sandwiches. Cut sandwiches in half and serve warm

CHAPTER 2
COOL SOUPS AND SANDWICHES

CHILLED ROASTED RED AND YELLOW PEPPER SOUP WITH AVOCADO SALSA

Prep: 20 min

Cooking: 10 min

Chill: 30 min

Serve: 4

NUTRITION:
Per serving: 160 calories, 9 g fat, 1.5 g saturated fat, 7 g protein, 12 g carbohydrate, 2 g fiber, 290 mg sodium

INGREDIENTS

Soup
- 1 tablespoon extra-virgin olive oil
- 1 large onion, chopped
- 1/4 teaspoon salt
- 2 cups lower-sodium chicken broth
- 2 roasted yellow peppers (from a jar), rinsed
- 2 roasted red peppers (from a jar), rinsed
- 1 cup low-fat or nonfat plain yogurt

Salsa
- 1/2 small avocado, finely chopped
- 1 tablespoon chopped fresh cilantro
- 1+1/2 teaspoons fresh lime juice

DIRECTION

1. For the soup: In a medium nonstick skillet, heat oil over medium heat; add onion and salt. Cook, stirring occasionally, until onion is softened, about 5 minutes. Add broth, bring to a boil, and simmer for 3 minutes; transfer to a medium bowl to cool.
2. Place half of the cooled broth mixture in a blender (make sure to get an equal amount of liquid and onions); add yellow peppers and 1/2 cup of the yogurt; purée until smooth. Transfer yellow pepper purée to a covered container and refrigerate until chilled, about 30 minutes. Rinse blender and transfer remaining broth mixture to it. Add red peppers and remaining 1/2 cup yogurt; purée until smooth. Transfer red pepper purée to another covered container and refrigerate until chilled, about 30 minutes.
3. For the salsa: While soups are chilling, in a small bowl combine avocado, cilantro, and lime juice.
4. To serve the soup, simultaneously ladle a generous 1/2 cup of the yellow pepper soup and a generous 1/2 cup of the red pepper soup into each of 4 shallow bowls, allowing soups to meet in center. Garnish each with salsa and serve

INDIAN SPICED CHILLED TOMATO SOUP

Prep: 10 min Cooking: 20 min

Chill: 30 min Serve: 4

NUTRITION:
Per serving: 150 calories, 5 g fat, 1.5 g saturated fat, 6 g protein, 17 g carbohydrate, 2 g fiber, 600 mg sodium

INGREDIENTS

- 1 tablespoon extra-virgin olive oil
- 1 teaspoon ground cardamom
- 1 teaspoon ground cumin
- 1/4 teaspoon cayenne
- 1 onion, chopped
- 2 garlic cloves, minced
- 1/4 teaspoon salt
- 1 (28-ounce) can whole peeled tomatoes, with juices
- 1+1/3 cups low-fat or nonfat plain yogurt
- 1 tablespoon fresh lime juice

DIRECTION

1. In a large nonstick skillet, heat oil over medium-high heat. Add cardamom, cumin, and cayenne; cook, stirring, until fragrant, about 30 seconds. Stir in onion, garlic, and salt; reduce the heat to medium and cook until onion is softened, about 5 minutes.
2. Add tomatoes and their juices, bring to a simmer, and cook for 10 minutes. Remove from the heat. Cool briefly and then stir in yogurt and lime juice.
3. Transfer half of the tomato mixture to a blender and purée until smooth; pour into a large bowl. Repeat with remaining tomato mixture; pour into the bowl.
4. Cover and refrigerate until chilled, about 30 minutes. Serve chilled.

CURRIED SUMMER SQUASH SOUP

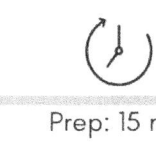
Prep: 15 min

Cooking: 15 min

Chill: 45 min

Serve: 4

NUTRITION:
Per serving: 200 calories, 5 g fat, 0.5 g saturated fat, 10 g protein, 30 g carbohydrate, 6 g fiber, 690 mg sodium

INGREDIENTS

- 1 tablespoon extra-virgin olive oil
- 2 teaspoons curry powder
- 2 medium yellow squash, chopped (3 cups)
- 1 large onion, coarsely chopped
- 3 cups lower-sodium chicken broth
- 1 (15.5-ounce) can chickpeas, rinsed and drained
- Salt and freshly ground black pepper
- 1/2 cup low-fat or nonfat plain yogurt
- 2 tablespoons chopped fresh basil

DIRECTION

1. In a large saucepan, heat oil over medium-high heat. Add curry powder and cook, stirring, until fragrant, about 30 seconds. Stir in squash and onion, cover, and reduce the heat to medium. Cook, stirring occasionally, until squash is softened, about 8 minutes.
2. Add broth and chickpeas, bring to a simmer, and remove from the heat. Transfer 2 cups of the soup to a blender and purée until smooth. Return puréed soup to the pan with the rest of the soup and stir to combine. Season with salt and pepper to taste.
3. Transfer soup to a covered container and refrigerate until chilled, about 45 minutes.
4. Divide soup among 4 bowls, top with a dollop of yogurt and a sprinkling of basil, and serve

SUMMERY MELON SOUP

Prep: 20 min

Cooking: 0 min

Chill: 30 min

Serve: 4

NUTRITION:
Per serving: 110 calories, 1 g fat, 0 g saturated fat, 3 g protein, 24 g carbohydrate, 2 g fiber, 60 mg sodium

INGREDIENTS

- 1/2 (5-pound) honeydew, peeled and chopped (5 cups)
- 1 large cucumber, peeled and chopped
- 1/2 cup low-fat or nonfat plain yogurt
- 2 scallions, roughly chopped
- 1 tablespoon fresh lemon juice
- 2 teaspoons finely grated lemon zest

DIRECTION

1. In a blender, purée honeydew until smooth. Add cucumber, yogurt, scallions, lemon juice, and 1 teaspoon of the zest; purée until smooth. Transfer soup to a covered container and refrigerate until chilled, about 30 minutes.
2. Divide soup among 4 bowls and sprinkle with remaining 1 teaspoon zest.

SWEET POTATO VICHYSSOISE

Prep: 15 min

Cooking: 20 min

Chill: 45 min

Serve: 4

NUTRITION:
Per serving: 160 calories, 4 g fat, 0.5 g saturated fat, 7 g protein, 24 g carbohydrate, 3 g fiber, 360 mg sodium

INGREDIENTS

- 2 medium sweet potatoes (1+1/2 pounds), peeled and cut into 1-inch chunks
- 1 tablespoon extra-virgin olive oil
- 2 medium leeks, roots and tops trimmed and discarded, whites chopped (3 cups)
- 1 cup lower-sodium chicken broth
- 2 cups fat-free milk
- 1/4 teaspoon salt
- 1 tablespoon chopped chives

DIRECTION

1. Place sweet potatoes in a medium saucepan and add water to cover. Bring to a low boil and cook until sweet potatoes have softened, about 15 minutes. Drain in a colander and let cool briefly.
2. While sweet potatoes are cooking, in a medium nonstick skillet heat oil over medium heat. Add leeks, cover, and cook until softened, about 5 minutes. Add broth, bring to a simmer, and cook for 3 minutes more. Remove from the heat and let cool briefly.
3. In a blender, combine sweet potatoes, leeks, and broth; purée for 1 minute. Add milk and salt; purée until smooth. Transfer soup to a covered container and refrigerate until chilled, about 45 minutes.
4. Divide soup among 4 bowls, sprinkle with chives, and serve.

CUCUMBER SOUP WITH GRILLED SHRIMP AND DILL

Prep: 20 min

Cooking: 5 min

Serve: 4

NUTRITION:
Per serving: 140 calories, 2.5 g fat, 1 g saturated fat, 19 g protein, 9 g carbohydrate, 1 g fiber, 300 mg sodium

INGREDIENTS

- 2 large cucumbers, peeled and roughly chopped
- 3/4 cup cold water
- 1 cup low-fat or nonfat plain yogurt
- 1 tablespoon fresh lime juice
- 1/4 teaspoon salt
- 1/4 teaspoon freshly ground black pepper
- 3/4 pound large shrimp, peeled and deveined
- 1/4 cup chopped fresh dill

DIRECTION

1. In a blender, combine cucumbers and water; purée for 30 seconds. Add yogurt, lime juice, salt, and pepper; purée until smooth.
2. Lightly coat a grill or grill pan with cooking spray and heat to medium-high. Grill shrimp just until pink, about 1 minute per side.
3. Divide soup among 4 bowls, top with shrimp and dill, and serve.

HEIRLOOM TOMATO GAZPACHO

 Prep: 25 min

 Cooking: 5 min

 Chill: 30 min

 Serve: 4

NUTRITION:

Per serving: 100 calories, 4.5 g fat, 0.5 g saturated fat, 3 g protein, 16 g carbohydrate, 4 g fiber, 170 mg sodium

INGREDIENTS

- 2 pounds heirloom tomatoes, roughly chopped, plus 1 contrasting-color heirloom tomato for garnish
- 1 garlic clove, roughly chopped
- 1 large cucumber, peeled and roughly chopped
- 1 medium green bell pepper, roughly chopped
- 1/3 cup parsley leaves
- 1/2 small red onion, roughly chopped
- 1 small jalapeño, seeded and roughly chopped
- 1 cup ice cubes
- 1 tablespoon extra-virgin olive oil
- 1 tablespoon red wine vinegar
- 1/4 teaspoon salt

DIRECTION

1. In a blender, combine 2 pounds tomatoes and garlic; purée until smooth. Transfer to a large bowl. In the blender, combine cucumber, bell pepper, parsley, onion, jalapeño, and ice; purée to a slightly chunky texture.
2. Add to the bowl with tomato mixture. Stir in oil, vinegar, and salt. Transfer gazpacho to a covered container and refrigerate until chilled, about 30 minutes. Just before serving, cut remaining tomato into small dice.
3. Divide gazpacho among 4 shallow bowls, top with diced tomato, and serve.

WHITE GAZPACHO

Prep: 15 min

Cooking: 5 min

Chill: 30 min

Serve: 4

NUTRITION:
Per serving: 150 calories, 9 g fat, 0.5 g saturated fat, 6 g protein, 14 g carbohydrate, 4 g fiber, 210 mg sodium

INGREDIENTS

- 1 slice whole-grain bread, crust removed
- 1+1/2 cups vegetable broth
- 1/2 cup slivered almonds
- 1 large cucumber, peeled and chopped
- 1 medium yellow bell pepper, chopped
- 4 scallions, chopped
- 1 tablespoon red wine vinegar
- 6 seedless green grapes, halved

DIRECTION

1. Place bread in a blender and cover with broth; let sit until bread begins to soften, about 3 minutes.
2. Reserve 2 tablespoons of the almonds; add remaining 6 tablespoons almonds to the blender and purée until very smooth, about 1 minute. Add cucumber, pepper, scallions, and vinegar to the blender; purée until mixture is slightly chunky.
3. Transfer soup to a covered container and refrigerate until chilled, about 30 minutes. To serve, divide soup among 4 bowls and top with reserved almonds and grape halves

GARDEN WHITE BEAN SOUP

 Prep: 25 min

 Cooking: 25 min

 Serve: 4

NUTRITION:
Per serving: 290 calories, 8 g fat, 2 g saturated fat, 17 g protein, 40 g carbohydrate, 9 g fiber, 660 mg sodium

INGREDIENTS

- 1 tablespoon plus 2 teaspoons extra-virgin olive oil
- 1 medium onion, thinly sliced
- 4 garlic cloves, thinly sliced
- 1 celery stalk, thinly sliced
- Pinch red pepper flakes
- 2 (15-ounce) cans Great Northern or cannellini beans, rinsed and drained
- 3 cups lower-sodium chicken broth
- 1+1/2 cups packed chopped arugula
- 1/4 cup packed basil leaves, roughly chopped
- 1/4 teaspoon grated lemon zest
- 1/4 teaspoon salt
- 4 tablespoons freshly grated Parmesan cheese

DIRECTION

1. In a medium saucepan, heat 1 tablespoon of the oil over medium heat. Add onion, garlic, celery, and pepper flakes. Reduce the heat to medium-low and cook, stirring occasionally, until vegetables are softened, 10 to 12 minutes. Add beans and broth, bring to a simmer, and cook for 10 minutes. Remove from the heat and carefully strain liquid into a large bowl.
2. Transfer bean mixture to a blender or food processor, add 1 cup of the reserved liquid, remaining 2 teaspoons oil, arugula, basil, lemon zest, and salt; purée until smooth. Add to the bowl with the rest of the reserved cooking liquid and stir to combine.
3. Ladle soup into 4 bowls, sprinkle evenly with cheese, and serve warm.

SAVORY EGG SALAD SANDWICHES

 Prep: 15 min

 Cooking: 10 min

 Stand time: 20 min

 Serve: 4

NUTRITION:
Per serving with bread: 270 calories, 16 g fat, 3 g saturated fat, 15 g protein, 16 g carbohydrate, 5 g fiber, 500 mg sodium

INGREDIENTS

- 8 large eggs
- 1/2 small red onion, minced
- 2 celery stalks, minced
- 4 large green olives, chopped (optional)
- 3 tablespoons mayonnaise
- 1 teaspoon Dijon mustard
- 1/4 teaspoon salt
- 4 slices whole-grain bread, toasted (optional)
- 1+1/2 cups baby arugula

DIRECTION

1. Place eggs in a medium saucepan, cover with water, and bring to a boil. Remove from the heat, cover, and let eggs sit for 20 minutes. Drain and place eggs in a bowl filled with ice water. When cool enough to handle, peel eggs. In a medium bowl, mash 5 whole eggs and 3 egg whites together with the back of a fork.
2. Add onion, celery, olives, if using, mayonnaise, mustard, and salt; stir to combine.
3. Cover bread slices, if using, evenly with arugula, top with egg salad, and serve open face.

PAN BAGNAT

Prep: 30 min

Cooking: 15 min

Marinating: 30 min

Serve: 4

NUTRITION:

Per serving: 410 calories, 12 g fat, 1.5 g saturated fat, 31 g protein, 40 g carbohydrate, 4 g fiber, 880 mg sodium

INGREDIENTS

- 4 ounces green beans, trimmed and cut into 1-inch pieces
- 1 tablespoon extra-virgin olive oil
- 1 teaspoon Dijon mustard
- 1 teaspoon red wine vinegar
- 1 (12-ounce) loaf whole-wheat peasant bread
- 2 (6-ounce) cans water-packed chunk light tuna, drained and flaked
- 2 medium plum tomatoes, sliced
- 2 hard-boiled eggs, sliced
- 8 kalamata olives, pitted and sliced

DIRECTION

1. Bring a medium saucepan of salted water to a boil. Add beans, return to a boil, and cook until crisp-tender, about 2 minutes. Drain in a colander and rinse under very cold water to stop cooking. Drain again and pat dry.
2. In a small bowl, whisk together oil, mustard, and vinegar.
3. Slice bread in half horizontally and then tear out the inner bread from both halves, leaving a 1/2-inch shell of bread in each half (use the torn-out bread for making bread crumbs). Layer tuna, tomatoes, eggs, green beans, and olives in the bottom half of the bread; drizzle with oil mixture. Place top on sandwich and wrap tightly with plastic wrap.
4. Compress sandwich by placing a heavy skillet on top of it. Let it sit, weighted down, for 30 minutes at room temperature. Remove from plastic wrap, cut into 4 wedges, and serve

GRILLED SALMON SALAD SANDWICHES

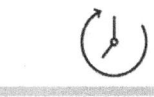
Prep: 15 min

Cooking: 12 min

Serve: 4

NUTRITION:
Per serving with bread: 310 calories, 14 g fat, 3 g saturated fat, 28 g protein, 19 g carbohydrate, 5 g fiber, 250 mg sodium

INGREDIENTS

- 1 pound skinless salmon fillet, about 1 inch thick
- 1+1/2 cups watercress leaves, chopped
- 1 medium cucumber, peeled and chopped
- 2 tablespoons reduced-fat sour cream
- 1 tablespoon fresh lemon juice
- 1 tablespoon chopped fresh dill
- 8 slices thin-sliced whole-wheat bread (optional)

DIRECTION

1. Lightly coat a grill or grill pan with cooking spray and heat to medium-high. Grill salmon until opaque in the center, 4 to 5 minutes per side. Transfer to a plate to cool.
2. In a large bowl, combine watercress, cucumber, sour cream, lemon juice, and dill. Using a fork, flake cooled salmon into the bowl; toss well.
3. Divide salad among 4 bread slices, if using, and cover with remaining bread. Cut in half and serve

SOUTH BEACH DIET CLUB SANDWICHES

 Prep: 15 min

 Cooking: 5 min

 Serve: 4

NUTRITION:
Per serving: 250 calories, 12 g fat, 2 g saturated fat, 19 g protein, 22 g carbohydrate, 7 g fiber, 630 mg sodium

INGREDIENTS

- 2 tablespoons mayonnaise
- 1 tablespoon fresh lemon juice
- 1/2 teaspoon ground cumin
- 1/4 teaspoon cayenne
- 4 slices Canadian bacon (about 1 ounce each)
- 8 slices thin-sliced whole-grain bread, lightly toasted
- 4 small red leaf lettuce leaves
- 1/4 pound thinly sliced salt-free or reduced-sodium deli turkey breast
- 1/2 small avocado, cut into 4 slices
- 1 large beefsteak tomato, cut into 4 slices

DIRECTION

1. In a small bowl, combine mayonnaise, lemon juice, cumin, and cayenne.
2. Lightly coat a large nonstick skillet with cooking spray and heat over medium-high heat. Add bacon and cook until edges begin to brown, about 1 minute per side. Transfer to a paper towel-lined plate.
3. Spread mayonnaise mixture on 4 toast slices. Top each with 1 lettuce leaf, one-fourth of the turkey, 1 avocado slice, 1 bacon slice, and 1 tomato slice; cover with remaining toast. Cut in half, secure with toothpicks, if necessary, and serve.

MEDITERRANEAN VEGETABLE SANDWICHES

 Prep: 25 min

 Cooking: 5 min

 Serve: 4

NUTRITION:
Per serving with pita: 290 calories, 9 g fat, 2.5 g saturated fat, 13 g protein, 44 g carbohydrate, 8 g fiber, 770 mg sodium

INGREDIENTS
- 1/2 small red onion, very thinly sliced
- 1 (15.5-ounce) can chickpeas, rinsed and drained
- 1+1/2 cups baby spinach
- 3 ounces reduced-fat feta cheese, crumbled (generous 1/3 cup)
- 1 medium cucumber, halved crosswise and thinly sliced lengthwise
- 1 large tomato, thinly sliced
- 2 roasted red peppers (from a jar), rinsed and cut into 1/4-inch slices
- 1/4 cup pitted kalamata olives, roughly chopped
- 1 tablespoon extra-virgin olive oil
- 1+1/2 teaspoons red wine vinegar
- 1/8 teaspoon ground cumin
- Cayenne
- 2 (6-inch) whole-grain pita breads, halved

DIRECTION
1. Place onion in a small bowl and cover with ice water; let sit for 10 minutes.
2. Drain onion, pat dry, and place in a medium bowl. Add chickpeas, spinach, feta, cucumber, tomato, peppers, olives, oil, vinegar, and cumin; stir gently to combine. Season with cayenne to taste.
3. Fill pita halves with vegetable mixture and serve.

CLASSIC LOBSTER ROLLS

Prep: 15 min
Cooking: 15 min
Serve: 4

NUTRITION:
Per serving with roll: 300 calories, 6 g fat, 1 g saturated fat, 36 g protein, 23 g carbohydrate, 3 g fiber, 880 mg sodium

INGREDIENTS

- 4 frozen lobster tails, defrosted (about 1+1/2 pounds)
- 1 small celery stalk, finely chopped
- 1 tablespoon minced red onion
- 1 tablespoon mayonnaise
- 1 tablespoon chopped tarragon leaves
- 1 teaspoon fresh lemon juice
- 1/4 teaspoon salt
- Freshly ground black pepper
- 4 whole-wheat hot dog rolls, lightly toasted (optional)

DIRECTION

1. Fill a large saucepan with enough water to come 1/2 inch up the side of the pan; cover and bring to a simmer. Add lobster tails, return to a simmer, and partially cover. Cook until lobster is opaque throughout, about 8 minutes. Remove lobster from the pan and let cool. When cool enough to handle, remove shells and chop lobster meat into bite-size pieces.
2. In a medium bowl, combine lobster, celery, onion, mayonnaise, tarragon, lemon juice, and salt. Season with pepper to taste. Divide lobster salad among 4 rolls, if using, and serve.

MONKFISH AND SHRIMP ROLLS

Prep: 25 min Cooking: 15 min Serve: 4

NUTRITION:
Per serving with roll: 300 calories, 10 g fat, 1.5 g saturated fat, 24 g protein, 32 g carbohydrate, 6 g fiber, 480 mg sodium

INGREDIENTS

- 1 seedless orange
- 1 lemon
- 1 lime
- 1 (8-ounce) monkfish fillet
- 1/2 pound large shrimp, peeled and deveined
- 1/2 small avocado, chopped
- 1 tablespoon mayonnaise
- 1/4 teaspoon salt
- 12 small spinach leaves, thinly sliced
- 4 whole-wheat hot dog rolls, lightly toasted (optional)

DIRECTION

1. Finely grate zest from orange, lemon, and lime over a small bowl; stir to combine. Place 1 teaspoon of the mixed zest in a medium bowl and place remaining zest in a medium skillet. Remove skin and white membrane from orange and chop the fruit. Add chopped orange to the bowl with zest.
2. Halve the lemon and lime and squeeze juice from both halves into the skillet. Add enough water to come 1/2 inch up the side of the pan, cover, and bring to a simmer. Add monkfish, return to a simmer, and cook, partially covered, until opaque in the center, about 5 minutes per side. Using a slotted spoon, transfer fish to a cutting board and cut into small chunks.
3. Bring liquid in the skillet back to a simmer, add shrimp, and simmer until shrimp turn pink, 1 to 2 minutes. Transfer shrimp to the cutting board and slice lengthwise. Add shrimp and monkfish to the bowl with orange mixture. Add avocado, mayonnaise, and salt; toss gently to combine.
4. Divide spinach leaves among rolls, if using, spoon salad evenly on top, and serve.

COOL COD SANDWICHES WITH HOMEMADE TARTAR SAUCE

Prep: 10 min

Cooking: 15 min

Serve: 4

NUTRITION:
Per serving with bun: 380 calories, 13 g fat, 2 g saturated fat, 37 g protein, 27 g carbohydrate, 3 g fiber, 650 mg sodium

INGREDIENTS

Sauce
- 2 tablespoons mayonnaise
- 2 tablespoons chopped cornichons
- 2 teaspoons capers, rinsed, drained, and chopped
- 1 tablespoon fresh lemon juice half

Sandwich
- 4 (6-ounce) cod fillets, about 1 inch thick
- 1/8 teaspoon salt
- 1 tablespoon extra-virgin olive oil
- 2 romaine lettuce leaves, torn in
- 4 whole-grain sandwich buns, lightly toasted (optional)

DIRECTION

1. For the sauce: In a small bowl, combine mayonnaise, cornichons, capers, and lemon juice.
2. For the sandwich: Sprinkle cod with salt. In a large nonstick skillet, heat oil over medium-high heat. Add cod and cook until golden on the outside and opaque inside, 4 to 5 minutes per side. Place lettuce and cod on buns, if using, dollop each with 1 tablespoon tartar sauce, and serve.

CHIPOTLE-RUBBED STEAK WRAPS

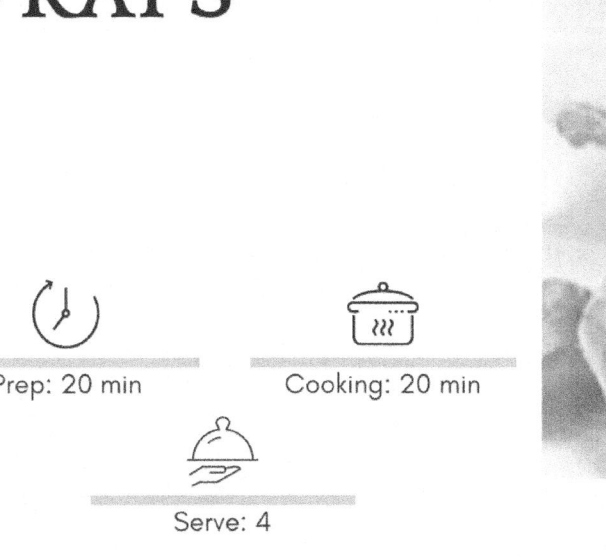

Prep: 20 min

Cooking: 20 min

Serve: 4

NUTRITION:

Per serving: 360 calories, 15 g fat, 5 g saturated fat, 36 g protein, 27 g carbohydrate, 8 g fiber, 580 mg sodium

INGREDIENTS

- 1 tablespoon chopped chipotle chiles in adobo, or more to taste
- 1 (1+1/4-pound) flank steak, about 1 inch thick
- 2 large romaine lettuce leaves, shredded
- 2 medium plum tomatoes, chopped
- 1 tablespoon reduced-fat sour cream
- 2 teaspoons fresh lime juice
- 1/4 teaspoon salt
- 4 (8-inch) whole-wheat wraps

DIRECTION

1. Rub chiles onto both sides of steak; place steak in a resealable plastic bag and let marinate at room temperature for 1 hour.
2. Heat the broiler and broiler pan for 10 minutes.
3. Place steak on broiler pan and cook for 4 to 5 minutes per side for medium-rare. Remove from the broiler, transfer to a cutting board, and let steak rest for 5 minutes.
4. Cut into thin slices across the grain. In a medium bowl, combine lettuce, tomatoes, sour cream, lime juice, and salt. Heat wraps in the oven or microwave according to package directions.
5. Divide lettuce mixture and steak evenly among wraps, roll up, and serve

CHAPTER 3
SUNSATIONAL SALADS AND SIDES

GREEN AND YELLOW BEANS WITH FRESH MOZZARELLA AND PINE NUTS

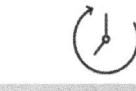
Prep: 10 min

Cooking: 10 min

Serve: 4

NUTRITION:
Per serving: 180 calories, 13 g fat, 5 g saturated fat, 8 g protein, 9 g carbohydrate, 4 g fiber, 190 mg sodium

INGREDIENTS

- 2 tablespoons pine nuts
- 8 ounces green beans, trimmed
- 8 ounces yellow wax beans, trimmed
- 1 tablespoon extra-virgin olive oil
- 1/4 teaspoon salt
- 1/8 teaspoon freshly ground black pepper
- 4 ounces fresh part-skim mozzarella cheese
- 1/4 cup basil leaves, sliced

DIRECTION

1. Heat the oven to 275°F. Spread pine nuts on a baking sheet and toast until fragrant and lightly golden, 5 to 7 minutes. Set aside.
2. While pine nuts are toasting, bring a large saucepan of water to a boil. Add beans and cook just until crisp-tender, about 3 minutes. Drain in a colander and run under very cold water for 1 minute to stop cooking. Drain again and pat dry. Transfer beans to a medium bowl and toss with oil, salt, and pepper.
3. Slice cheese into 4 thin slices and cut each slice in half so that you have 8 half-circles. Divide cheese slices and beans among 4 salad plates, alternating the green and yellow beans with the cheese slices. Sprinkle with basil and pine nuts and serve.

SEAFOOD CAESAR

Prep: 20 min

Cooking: 8 min

Serve: 4

NUTRITION:
Per serving: 207 calories, 12 g fat, 2 g saturated fat, 20 g protein, 5 g carbohydrate, 2 g fiber, 391 mg sodium

INGREDIENTS

- 3/4 pound large shrimp (about 16), peeled and deveined
- 2 teaspoons plus 2 tablespoons extra-virgin olive oil
- 2 garlic cloves, minced
- 1 teaspoon grated lemon zest
- 1/4 teaspoon freshly ground black pepper
- 2 teaspoons fresh lemon juice
- 4 anchovy fillets, minced, or 2 teaspoons anchovy paste
- 1 teaspoon Dijon mustard
- 1 (1-pound) head romaine lettuce, chopped (8 cups)
- 1 tablespoon freshly grated Parmesan cheese
- 1/2 pound lump crabmeat (about 1 cup)

DIRECTION

1. In a medium bowl, toss shrimp with 2 teaspoons of the oil, half of the garlic, lemon zest, and pepper.
2. Lightly coat a grill or grill pan with cooking spray and heat to medium-high. Grill shrimp until they turn pink, 2 to 3 minutes per side. Remove from the heat and set aside. In a large bowl, whisk together lemon juice, anchovies, mustard, and remaining garlic. Slowly whisk in remaining 2 tablespoons oil.
3. Add lettuce and cheese and toss well. Divide lettuce among 4 plates, top with shrimp and crab, and serve.

POACHED CHICKEN, ZUCCHINI, AND WHEAT BERRY SALAD

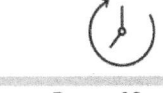 Prep: 10 min   Cooking: 50 min

 Serve: 4

NUTRITION:
Per serving: 260 calories, 5 g fat, 1 g saturated fat, 33 g protein, 22 g carbohydrate, 4 g fiber, 460 mg sodium

INGREDIENTS
- 1/2 cup soft wheat berries
- 1+3/4 cups lower-sodium chicken broth
- 1 pound boneless, skinless chicken breasts
- Freshly ground black pepper
- 1+1/2 cups water
- 3 teaspoons fresh lemon juice
- 1 medium zucchini, peeled into thin strips
- 1/2 cup nonfat plain yogurt
- 1 tablespoon extra-virgin olive oil
- 1/8 teaspoon salt
- 4 large Boston lettuce leaves
- 1/4 cup basil leaves, thinly sliced

DIRECTION
1. Place wheat berries in a medium saucepan and cover with about 2 inches of water. Bring to a boil over medium-high heat, turn off the heat, and cover. Let stand for 15 to 20 minutes.
2. Drain and return wheat berries to the pan. Add broth and bring to a boil over medium-high heat. Reduce the heat, cover, and simmer until the broth is absorbed and the berries are firm but not crunchy, 40 to 45 minutes
3. Transfer wheat berries to a large bowl.
4. While wheat berries are cooking, lightly season chicken with pepper. In a large nonstick skillet, combine chicken, water, and 1 teaspoon of the lemon juice; bring to a simmer over medium heat. Reduce the heat to low, cover, and simmer until chicken is cooked through, 10 to 15 minutes, turning once halfway through cooking. Remove chicken from liquid, transfer to a cutting board, and when cool enough to handle, cut into 1/2-inch cubes. Add chicken and zucchini to the bowl with cooked wheat berries.
5. In a small bowl, whisk together yogurt, oil, salt, and remaining 2 teaspoons lemon juice. Pour dressing over chicken mixture and toss to combine. Divide lettuce leaves among 4 salad plates. Spoon chicken mixture onto lettuce, sprinkle with basil, and serve.

SUMMER'S BOUNTY GREEK SALAD

Prep: 15 min

Cooking: 15 min

Serve: 4

NUTRITION:
Per serving: 180 calories, 12 g fat, 3 g saturated fat, 9 g protein, 13 g carbohydrate, 6 g fiber, 550 mg sodium

INGREDIENTS

- 8 ounces green beans, trimmed
- 1 (12-ounce) head romaine lettuce, chopped (6 cups)
- 2 medium tomatoes, cut into wedges
- 1 medium cucumber, halved lengthwise, seeded, and thinly sliced
- 4 ounces reduced-fat feta cheese, crumbled (2/3 cup)
- 1/4 cup pitted kalamata olives, sliced
- 2 tablespoons extra-virgin olive oil
- 1 tablespoon red wine vinegar
- 1/8 teaspoon salt
- 1/8 teaspoon freshly ground black pepper
- 1/4 cup chopped fresh parsley

DIRECTION

1. Bring a large saucepan of lightly salted water to a boil. Add beans and cook just until crisp-tender, about 3 minutes. Drain in a colander and run under very cold water for 1 minute to stop cooking. Drain again and pat dry. Cut beans into 1-inch pieces.
2. In a large bowl, combine beans, lettuce, tomatoes, cucumber, feta, and olives. In a small bowl, whisk together oil, vinegar, salt, and pepper; pour over salad and toss to coat. Divide salad among 4 plates and sprinkle with parsley just before serving.

ENDIVE SALAD WITH WALNUTS

Prep: 10 min | Cooking: 10 min | Serve: 4

NUTRITION:
Per serving: 130 calories, 12 g fat, 1.5 g saturated fat, 3 g protein, 6 g carbohydrate, 4 g fiber, 160 mg sodium

INGREDIENTS

- 1/2 cup walnut halves
- 1 tablespoon extra-virgin olive oil
- 1 teaspoon Dijon mustard
- 1 teaspoon red wine vinegar
- 4 heads Belgian endive (1 pound)
- 1/4 teaspoon salt
- 1/8 teaspoon freshly ground black pepper

DIRECTION

1. Heat the oven to 350°F. Spread walnuts on a baking sheet and toast until fragrant and lightly browned, about 10 minutes.
2. In a large bowl, whisk together oil, mustard, and vinegar. Trim endives, halve each head lengthwise, then cut lengthwise into long, thin strips. Add endive, walnuts, salt, and pepper to the bowl with dressing; toss to combine. Divide salad among 4 salad plates and serve

HONEYDEW, FRESH HERB, AND RICOTTA SALATA SALAD

 Prep: 10 min

 Cooking: 10 min

 Serve: 4

NUTRITION:
Per serving: 160 calories, 8 g fat, 3 g saturated fat, 4 g protein, 20 g carbohydrate, 2 g fiber, 420 mg sodium

INGREDIENTS

- 1 (4- to 5-pound) honeydew melon, scooped into balls (4 cups)
- 1 cucumber, peeled and thinly sliced
- 1 tablespoon plus
- 1 teaspoon extra-virgin olive oil
- 1+1/2 teaspoons red wine vinegar
- 1/4 teaspoon salt
- 1/8 teaspoon freshly ground black pepper
- 1/4 cup packed basil leaves, thinly sliced
- 2 tablespoons chopped fresh parsley
- 2 ounces ricotta salata cheese

DIRECTION

1. In a large bowl, combine melon and cucumber. In a small bowl, whisk together oil, vinegar, salt, and pepper; pour over melon and cucumber and toss to coat. Add basil and parsley and toss to combine. Divide salad among 4 bowls, cups, or plates, shave cheese over the top, and serve.

CRISP JÍCAMA SALAD WITH CREAMY CILANTRO DRESSING

Prep: 15 min Cooking: 0 min Serve: 4

NUTRITION:
Per serving: 130 calories, 7 g fat, 1 g saturated fat, 4 g protein, 13 g carbohydrate, 1 g fiber, 190 mg sodium

INGREDIENTS

- 1/2 cup nonfat or low-fat plain yogurt
- 1/4 cup finely chopped fresh cilantro
- 3 tablespoons fresh lime juice
- 2 tablespoons extra-virgin olive oil
- 1/4 teaspoon salt
- 1/8 teaspoon freshly ground black pepper
- 1 (10-ounce) head red leaf lettuce, chopped (6 cups)
- 1 (1-pound) jícama, peeled and cut into matchsticks
- 1 medium cucumber, seeded and thinly sliced

DIRECTION

1. In a small bowl, combine yogurt, cilantro, lime juice, oil, salt, and pepper. Place lettuce in a large bowl and toss with 1/4 cup of the dressing; divide among 4 salad plates. Add jícama and cucumber to the same large bowl and toss with remaining dressing. Spoon jícama and cucumber mixture on top of lettuce and serve.

ROMAINE HEARTS WITH TUNA, EDAMAME, AND GREEN GODDESS DRESSING

Prep: 15 min

Cooking: 0 min

Serve: 4

NUTRITION:
Per serving: 280 calories, 15 g fat, 2.5 g saturated fat, 27 g protein, 9 g carbohydrate, 4 g fiber, 500 mg sodium

INGREDIENTS

- 1/2 medium avocado
- 3 tablespoons mayonnaise
- 3 tablespoons nonfat or low-fat plain yogurt
- 1 tablespoon water
- 2 scallions, chopped
- 1 small garlic clove
- 2 tablespoons chopped fresh basil
- 1 tablespoon chopped fresh parsley
- 1 tablespoon chopped fresh tarragon
- 2 teaspoons fresh lemon juice
- 1/4 teaspoon salt
- 1/8 teaspoon freshly ground black pepper
- 3 romaine hearts, chopped (8 cups)
- 2 (6-ounce) cans water-packed chunk light tuna, drained and flaked
- 1 cup frozen shelled edamame, defrosted

DIRECTION

1. In a blender, combine avocado, mayonnaise, yogurt, water, scallions, and garlic; purée until smooth. Add basil, parsley, tarragon, lemon juice, salt, and pepper; blend just until combined. In a large bowl, combine romaine, tuna, and edamame. Add dressing and toss. Serve at room temperature.

GRILLED SOUTHWEST STEAK, RADISH, AND BLUE CHEESE SALAD

Prep: 15 min   Cooking: 10 min

Serve: 4

NUTRITION:
Per serving: 360 calories, 19 g fat, 8 g saturated fat, 39 g protein, 7 g carbohydrate, 3 g fiber, 680 mg sodium

INGREDIENTS

- 2 garlic cloves, minced
- 1 tablespoon chili powder
- 2 teaspoons ground cumin
- 1/4 teaspoon salt
- 1/4 teaspoon freshly ground black pepper
- 1+1/4 pounds lean sirloin steak, about 3/4 inch thick
- 1 (12-ounce) head romaine lettuce, chopped (6 cups)
- 8 large radishes, cut into wedges, plus whole radishes for garnish
- 4 ounces blue cheese, crumbled (1/2 cup)
- 1 tablespoon extra-virgin olive oil
- 1 tablespoon fresh lime juice

DIRECTION

1. In a small bowl, combine garlic, chili powder, cumin, 1/8 teaspoon of the salt, and 1/8 teaspoon of the pepper. Rub spice mixture onto steak.
2. Lightly coat a grill or grill pan with cooking spray and heat to medium-high. Grill steak about 4 minutes per side for medium-rare. Transfer to a cutting board and let rest for 5 minutes before cutting into thin slices. In a large bowl, combine lettuce, radishes, cheese, oil, lime juice, and remaining 1/8 teaspoon salt and 1/8 teaspoon pepper.
3. Divide salad among 4 plates, top with steak slices, and garnish with whole radishes. Serve warm.

BABY GREENS WITH TINY TOMATOES, FRESH HERBS, AND TOASTED PISTACHIOS

Prep: 15 min

Cooking: 10 min

Serve: 4

NUTRITION:
Per serving: 160 calories, 11 g fat, 1.5 g saturated fat, 6 g protein, 13 g carbohydrate, 5 g fiber, 180 mg sodium

INGREDIENTS

- 1/2 cup unsalted shelled pistachios
- 6 ounces mixed baby greens (6 cups)
- 1+1/2 cups cherry tomatoes, halved
- 1 medium cucumber, thinly sliced
- 1/4 cup basil leaves, roughly chopped
- 1/4 cup mint leaves, roughly chopped
- 1 tablespoon extra-virgin olive oil
- 2 teaspoons sherry vinegar
- 1/4 teaspoon salt
- 1/8 teaspoon freshly ground black pepper

DIRECTION

1. Heat the oven to 350°F. Spread pistachios on a baking sheet; toast until golden brown, about 8 minutes.
2. Transfer to a cutting board and roughly chop. In a large bowl, combine greens, tomatoes, cucumber, basil, and mint. Add oil, vinegar, salt, and pepper; toss to coat. Divide salad among 4 plates, sprinkle with pistachios, and serve

GRILLED ASPARAGUS WITH LEMON AIOLI

Prep: 10 min

Cooking: 10 min

Serve: 4

NUTRITION:
Per serving: 150 calories, 14 g fat, 2 g saturated fat, 3 g protein, 6 g carbohydrate, 3 g fiber, 240 mg sodium

INGREDIENTS

- 1/4 cup mayonnaise
- 1/2 teaspoon grated lemon zest
- 1 teaspoon fresh lemon juice
- 2 garlic cloves, minced
- 1/4 teaspoon salt
- 1/8 teaspoon freshly ground black pepper
- 1+1/2 pounds medium-thick asparagus, trimmed
- 2 teaspoons extra-virgin olive oil

DIRECTION

1. Lightly coat a grill or grill pan with cooking spray and heat to medium-high. In a small bowl, whisk together mayonnaise, lemon zest, lemon juice, garlic, 1/8 teaspoon of the salt, and pepper.
2. In a large bowl, toss asparagus with oil and remaining 1/8 teaspoon salt. Grill asparagus, turning occasionally, until lightly browned and tender, 8 to 10 minutes. Divide asparagus among 4 plates, spoon aioli on top, and serve.

MOROCCAN COUSCOUS

Prep: 10 min

Cooking: 10 min

Serve: 4

NUTRITION:
Per serving: 100 calories, 4 g fat, 0.5 g saturated fat, 3 g protein, 15 g carbohydrate, 3 g fiber, 150 mg sodium

INGREDIENTS

- 1/2 cup whole-wheat couscous
- 1+1/2 teaspoons ground cumin
- 1 teaspoon paprika
- 1/2 teaspoon ground cinnamon
- 1/4 teaspoon salt
- 1/8 teaspoon freshly ground black pepper
- Pinch cayenne
- 1 tomato, chopped
- 1/3 cup minced red onion
- 1 tablespoon extra-virgin olive oil
- 2 teaspoons fresh lemon juice
- 3 tablespoons minced fresh parsley

DIRECTION

1. Prepare couscous according to package directions.
2. In a small bowl, combine cumin, paprika, cinnamon, salt, pepper, and cayenne. Fluff cooked couscous with a fork.
3. Add cumin mixture, tomato, onion, oil, and lemon juice; stir to combine. Divide among 4 plates, sprinkle with parsley, and serve warm.

GRILLED EGGPLANT ROUNDS WITH GARLICKY CILANTRO TOPPING

Prep: 10 min   Cooking: 10 min

Serve: 4

NUTRITION:
Per serving: 60 calories, 0.5 g fat, 0 g saturated fat, 2 g protein, 13 g carbohydrate, 8 g fiber, 151 mg sodium

INGREDIENTS

- 1 tablespoon chili powder
- 1 teaspoon ground cumin
- 1/4 teaspoon salt
- 2 tablespoons finely chopped fresh cilantro, plus sprigs for garnish
- 1 garlic clove, minced
- 2 medium eggplants (about 2 pounds), cut into 20 (1/2-inch-thick) rounds

DIRECTION

1. Lightly coat a grill or grill pan with cooking spray and heat to medium-high.
2. In a small bowl, stir together chili powder, cumin, and salt. In another small bowl, stir together cilantro and garlic.
3. Using a sharp paring knife, score a crisscross pattern on both sides of eggplant rounds; season both sides of rounds with chili powder mixture.
4. Grill eggplant until softened, 4 to 5 minutes per side; transfer to a serving platter. Sprinkle eggplant with cilantro mixture, garnish with cilantro sprigs, and serve hot

PICNIC MACARONI SALAD

Prep: 10 min

Cooking: 20 min

Serve: 8

NUTRITION:
Per serving: 120 calories, 4.5 g fat, 1 g saturated fat, 4 g protein, 18 g carbohydrate, 3 g fiber, 105 mg sodium

INGREDIENTS

- 1+1/2 cups whole-wheat or spelt elbow pasta
- 2 medium tomatoes, chopped
- 1 medium red bell pepper, diced
- 1 medium carrot, diced
- 1/3 cup reduced-fat sour cream
- 1/4 cup chopped cornichons (optional)
- 2 tablespoons mayonnaise
- 1 teaspoon dried oregano
- 1/4 teaspoon salt
- 1/8 teaspoon freshly ground black pepper

DIRECTION

1. Bring a large pot of lightly salted water to a boil. Cook pasta according to package directions until al dente.
2. Drain, run under cold water to cool, and drain again. In a large bowl, combine pasta, tomatoes, bell pepper, carrot, sour cream, cornichons, if using, mayonnaise, oregano, salt, and black pepper. Serve at room temperature or chilled.

SUMMERTIME SWEET POTATO SALAD

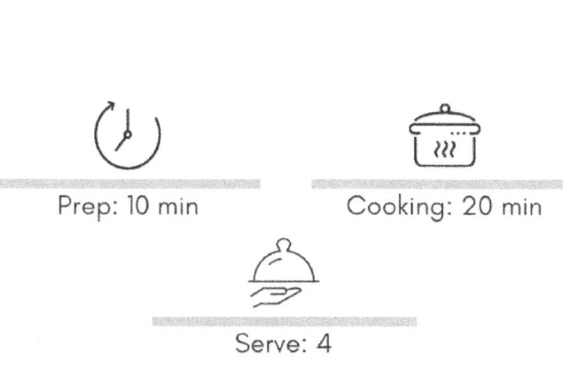

Prep: 10 min　　Cooking: 20 min

Serve: 4

NUTRITION:

Per serving: 120 calories, 0 g fat, 0 g saturated fat, 4 g protein, 27 g carbohydrate, 4 g fiber, 210 mg sodium

INGREDIENTS

- 2 medium sweet potatoes (1+1/2 pounds), peeled and cut into 1-inch cubes
- 1/3 cup nonfat or low-fat plain yogurt
- 1 small red bell pepper, diced
- 2 scallions, thinly sliced
- 3 tablespoons chopped fresh basil
- 1 teaspoon red wine vinegar
- 1/4 teaspoon salt
- 1/8 teaspoon freshly ground black pepper

DIRECTION

1. Place sweet potatoes in a medium saucepan and add cold water to cover. Bring to a boil and cook until tender, 8 to 10 minutes.
2. Drain, run under cold water to cool, and drain again. In a large bowl, combine sweet potatoes, yogurt, bell pepper, scallions, basil, vinegar, salt, and black pepper. Serve at room temperature or chilled

GRILLED FENNEL WITH MIXED OLIVES

Prep: 10 min

Cooking: 10 min

Serve: 4

NUTRITION:
Per serving: 90 calories, 6 g fat, 0.5 g saturated fat, 2 g protein, 10 g carbohydrate, 4 g fiber, 290 mg sodium

INGREDIENTS

- 2 large fennel bulbs, trimmed and cut lengthwise into 2-inch wedges (do not core)
- 1/8 teaspoon salt
- Pinch freshly ground black pepper
- 1/2 cup pitted mixed olives, roughly chopped
- 1 tablespoon extra-virgin olive oil
- 2 teaspoons grated lemon zest
- 1/2 teaspoons fresh lemon juice

DIRECTION

1. Lightly coat a grill or grill pan with cooking spray and heat to medium-high.
2. Season fennel with salt and pepper. Grill until tender, 4 to 5 minutes per side. Transfer fennel to a cutting board and remove any tough core from wedges.
3. In a large bowl, toss fennel with olives, oil, lemon zest, and lemon juice. Serve warm or at room temperature.

GRILLED CHIPOTLE ONION RING

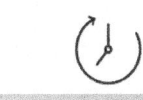
Prep: 10 min

Cooking: 12 min

Serve: 4

NUTRITION:
Per serving: 30 calories, 0 g fat, 0 g saturated fat, 1 g protein, 7 g carbohydrate, 1 g fiber, 150 mg sodium

INGREDIENTS

- 2 medium onions, cut into 1/2-inch-thick rounds
- 1/4 teaspoon salt
- 1/8 teaspoon freshly ground black pepper
- 2 canned chipotle chiles in adobo, rinsed, seeded, and minced
- 2 teaspoons fresh lime juice

DIRECTION

1. Lightly coat a grill or grill pan with cooking spray and heat to medium-high.
2. In a medium bowl, toss onions with salt and pepper (rings can separate).
3. Grill onions, turning occasionally, until lightly browned, 10 to 12 minutes.
4. Return onions to bowl, add chiles and lime juice, and toss until the onions are well coated. Serve warm.

SOUTHERN-STYLE GREENS

Prep: 10 min

Cooking: 15 min

Serve: 4

NUTRITION:
Per serving: 110 calories, 5 g fat, 1 g saturated fat, 5 g protein, 12 g carbohydrate, 2 g fiber, 330 mg sodium

INGREDIENTS

- 2 teaspoons extra-virgin olive oil
- 3 slices turkey bacon, finely chopped
- 1 small onion, finely chopped
- 2 garlic cloves, minced
- 1 cup water
- 1 (1-pound) bunch kale, stemmed and thinly sliced (8 cups)
- 1/4 teaspoon salt
- 1/8 teaspoon freshly ground black pepper

DIRECTION

1. In a large nonstick skillet, heat oil over medium heat. Add bacon and cook until browned and crisp, 3 to 5 minutes. Remove bacon from the skillet with a slotted spoon and drain on paper towels.
2. Add onion and garlic to the skillet and cook, stirring occasionally, over medium heat until onion is softened, about 3 minutes. Add water and half of the kale; bring to a simmer, cover, and cook until kale is wilted, about 2 minutes.
3. Add remaining kale, salt, and pepper; cover and cook until kale is tender and water has evaporated, about 3 minutes more. Add bacon to the skillet; stir to combine with kale and heat through, about 30 seconds. Divide among 4 plates and serve warm.

SPICY GRILLED SWEET POTATO FRIES

Prep: 15 min

Cooking: 10 min

Serve: 4

NUTRITION:
Per serving: 200 calories, 7 g fat, 1 g saturated fat, 2 g protein, 32 g carbohydrate, 4 g fiber, 190 mg sodium

INGREDIENTS

- 4 medium sweet potatoes (about 1 pound), peeled
- 2 tablespoons extra-virgin olive oil
- 1 teaspoon paprika
- 1 teaspoon dried thyme
- 1/4 teaspoon salt
- 1/4 teaspoon cayenne
- 1/8 teaspoon freshly ground black pepper

DIRECTION

1. Lightly coat a grill or grill pan with cooking spray and heat to medium-high.
2. Cut sweet potatoes into fries 1/3 inch thick by 2 to 4 inches long. In a medium bowl, combine sweet potatoes, oil, paprika, thyme, salt, cayenne, and black pepper. Grill sweet potatoes, turning occasionally, until tender and lightly browned, 8 to 10 minutes. Transfer to a platter and serve hot.

SAVOY SLAW WITH SESAME DRESSING

Prep: 10 min

Cooking: 5 min

Serve: 4

NUTRITION:
Per serving: 70 calories, 4.5 g fat, 0.5 g saturated fat, 2 g protein, 7 g carbohydrate, 3 g fiber, 166 mg sodium

INGREDIENTS

- 1 tablespoon sesame seeds
- 1 (1+1/2-pound) Savoy cabbage, shredded (4 cups)
- 1 medium red bell pepper, cut into thin strips
- 1 tablespoon toasted sesame oil
- 2 teaspoons red wine vinegar
- 1/4 teaspoon salt
- 1/8 teaspoon freshly ground black pepper

DIRECTION

1. In a small skillet, toast sesame seeds over medium-low heat, shaking the pan occasionally, until seeds are golden, about 5 minutes.
2. Remove from the heat. In a large bowl, combine cabbage, bell pepper, sesame oil, vinegar, salt, and black pepper. Add sesame seeds and toss. Serve at room temperature.

SPANISH RICE SALAD WITH PUMPKIN SEEDS

Prep: 15 min

Cooking: 15 min

Serve: 4

NUTRITION:
Per serving: 170 calories, 7 g fat, 0.5 g saturated fat, 4 g protein, 25 g carbohydrate, 3 g fiber, 240 mg sodium

INGREDIENTS

- 1/2 cup quick-cooking whole-grain brown rice
- 2 medium tomatoes, finely chopped 1 small onion, finely chopped
- 1/2 cup pitted green olives, sliced lengthwise
- 1/4 cup pumpkin seeds
- 1 tablespoon extra-virgin olive oil
- 1 teaspoon sherry vinegar
- 1 teaspoon dried oregano
- 1/4 teaspoon salt
- 1/8 teaspoon freshly ground black pepper
- 2 tablespoons chopped fresh parsley

DIRECTION

1. Cook rice according to package directions. Remove from the heat, spread on a plate, and refrigerate until cooled to room temperature, about 5 minutes.
2. In a large bowl, combine rice, tomatoes, onion, olives, pumpkin seeds, oil, vinegar, oregano, salt, and pepper. Divide salad among 4 plates and sprinkle with parsley just before serving.

GREEN RICE WITH SUMMER PEAS

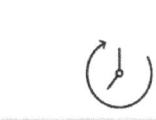 Prep: 20 min

 Cooking: 20 min

 Serve: 4

NUTRITION:
Per serving: 120 calories, 7 g fat, 1 g saturated fat, 3 g protein, 13 g carbohydrate, 2 g fiber, 150 mg sodium

INGREDIENTS

- 1/2 cup quick-cooking whole-grain brown rice
- 2 tablespoons water
- 1 tablespoon plus
- 2 teaspoons extra-virgin olive oil
- 1 tablespoon chopped fresh basil
- 1 tablespoon chopped fresh parsley
- 2 teaspoons chopped fresh mint
- 2 teaspoons chopped fresh tarragon
- 2 scallions, finely chopped
- 1 cup snow peas, trimmed
- 3/4 cup fresh or frozen peas
- 1/4 teaspoon salt
- Freshly ground black pepper

DIRECTION

1. Cook rice according to package directions. Remove from the heat and keep warm. While rice is cooking, in a blender combine water, 1 tablespoon of the oil, basil, parsley, mint, and tarragon; purée until smooth.
2. In a large nonstick skillet, heat remaining 2 teaspoons oil over medium heat. Add scallions and cook until fragrant, about 1 minute.
3. Add snow peas and regular peas and cook 2 minutes more. Add cooked rice and stir well to combine and heat through, about 1 minute more. Remove rice mixture from the heat, transfer to a serving bowl, and stir in herb mixture, salt, and pepper to taste.
4. Serve warm or at room temperature.

RED BEANS AND RICE

Prep: 10 min

Cooking: 20 min

Serve: 4

NUTRITION:

Per serving: 140 calories, 4.5 g fat, 0.5 g saturated fat, 5 g protein, 20 g carbohydrate, 4 g fiber, 400 mg sodium

INGREDIENTS

- 1/2 cup quick-cooking whole-grain brown rice
- 1 tablespoon extra-virgin olive oil
- 1 onion, finely chopped
- 1 (15-ounce) can red kidney beans, rinsed and drained
- 1/2 teaspoon dried thyme
- 1/4 teaspoon garlic powder
- 1/4 teaspoon hot pepper sauce, or more to taste
- 1/4 teaspoon salt
- 1/8 teaspoon freshly ground black pepper
- 1/8 teaspoon ground white pepper

DIRECTION

1. Cook rice according to package directions. Remove from the heat. In a large nonstick skillet, heat oil over medium heat. Add onion and cook until translucent and beginning to brown, 3 to 5 minutes.
2. Add rice, beans, thyme, garlic powder, hot pepper sauce, salt, black pepper, and white pepper; stir to combine. Cook until heated through, about 2 minutes. Serve hot.

CITRUSY HOT PEPPER SLAW

Prep: 20 min

Cooking: 0 min

Serve: 4

NUTRITION:
Per serving: 80 calories, 3.5 g fat, 0.5 g saturated fat, 2 g protein, 12 g carbohydrate, 4 g fiber, 160 mg sodium

INGREDIENTS

- 1 large seedless orange
- 1/2 (3-pound) green cabbage, shredded (6 cups)
- 2 medium jalapeños, seeded and minced
- 1 tablespoon fresh lemon juice
- 1 tablespoon extra-virgin olive oil
- 1/4 teaspoon salt
- 1/8 teaspoon freshly ground black pepper

DIRECTION

1. Finely grate zest from half of the orange over a medium bowl; set aside. Peel orange. Holding orange over a small bowl to catch juice, carefully cut along the membrane on both sides of each orange segment.
2. Allow the freed segments to fall into the bowl. Squeeze the remaining membrane over the bowl containing zest to extract any additional juice. Pour any juice from orange segments into the bowl with zest. Roughly chop orange segments and add them to the bowl with zest and juice.
3. Add cabbage, jalapeños, lemon juice, oil, salt, and pepper to the bowl with the orange; toss well. Serve at room temperature.

CHAPTER 4
FRESH FROM THE SEA

SOUTHERN-STYLE SHRIMP BOIL

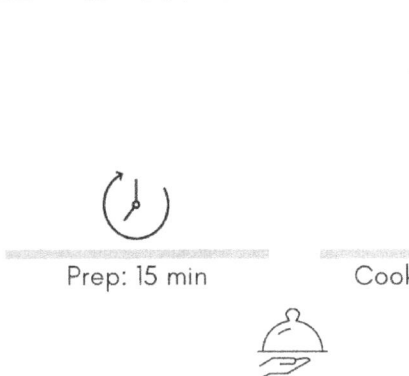

Prep: 15 min   Cooking: 20 min

Serve: 4

NUTRITION:
Per serving with corn: 250 calories, 5 g fat, 1 g saturated fat, 38 g protein, 13 g carbohydrate, 2 g fiber, 630 mg sodium

INGREDIENTS

- 2 tablespoons shrimp boil seasoning or crab boil seasoning
- 1 (4-ounce) low-fat hot Italian turkey sausage link, casing removed and sausage crumbled
- 2 ears of corn, shucked, each cut into 4 pieces
- 1 small red onion, cut into thin wedges
- 4 ounces green beans, trimmed and halved
- 1+1/2 pounds large unpeeled shrimp

DIRECTION

1. Fill a large saucepan with water to three-quarters full, add shrimp boil seasoning, and bring to a boil. Add sausage, corn, onion, and green beans; return to a simmer and cook for 5 minutes.
2. Add shrimp, return to a simmer, and cook until shrimp are pink, 2 to 3 minutes more.
3. Drain in a large colander. Divide shrimp boil among 4 shallow bowls and serve warm.

FRESH BLACKENED TUNA WITH GREENS

Prep: 5 min Cooking: 8 min Serve: 4

NUTRITION:
Per serving: 230 calories, 5 g fat, 1 g saturated fat, 41 g protein, 4 g carbohydrate, 2 g fiber, 500 mg sodium

INGREDIENTS

- 4 (6-ounce) tuna steaks or fillets, about 1+1/4 inches thick
- 1 tablespoon Cajun seasoning
- 1 tablespoon extra-virgin olive oil
- 1 teaspoon grated lemon zest
- 2 teaspoons fresh lemon juice
- 6 ounces mixed baby greens (6 cups)
- Salt and freshly ground black pepper

DIRECTION

1. Lightly coat a large cast-iron skillet with cooking spray and heat over mediumhigh heat. Rub each side of the tuna steaks with Cajun seasoning. Place steaks in the pan and cook until blackened, but not burned, on each side, about 3 minutes per side for medium-rare. Remove the pan from the heat.
2. In a large bowl, whisk together oil, lemon zest, and lemon juice. Add greens and toss to coat. Season with salt and pepper to taste and divide salad among 4 plates. Top each with a piece of blackened tuna and serve.

LEMONY POACHED HALIBUT WITH CREAMY CUCUMBERS

Prep: 20 min

Cooking: 15 min

Serve: 4

NUTRITION:
Per serving: 230 calories, 6 g fat, 1.5 g saturated fat, 37 g protein, 7 g carbohydrate, 2 g fiber, 250 mg sodium

INGREDIENTS

- 4 cups water
- 2 lemons, thinly sliced
- 3 medium shallots, thinly sliced
- 4 (6-ounce) pieces halibut fillet, skin removed
- 2 medium cucumbers, thinly sliced
- 3 tablespoons roughly chopped fresh dill
- 1/4 cup reduced-fat sour cream
- 1/4 teaspoon salt

DIRECTION

1. In a medium saucepan, bring water, lemons, and shallots to a simmer over medium-high heat. Add halibut, nestling fish pieces under lemons and shallots. Return water to a simmer and simmer gently until fish is opaque and tender, 5 to 8 minutes.
2. While fish is cooking, in a medium bowl combine cucumbers, dill, sour cream, and salt.
3. When fish is done, using a large slotted spoon, carefully transfer fish to 4 plates. Drain lemon and shallot slices and place on top of fish. Serve warm with cucumbers on the side.

SEAFOOD PAELLA

 Prep: 25 min

 Cooking: 25 min

 Serve: 4

NUTRITION:
Per serving: 320 calories, 9 g fat, 1.5 g saturated fat, 34 g protein, 23 g carbohydrate, 2 g fiber, 710 mg sodium

INGREDIENTS

- 1 tablespoon extra-virgin olive oil
- 1 (4-ounce) low-fat hot Italian turkey sausage link
- 1 medium onion, chopped
- 2 garlic cloves, sliced
- 1/3 cup white wine
- 1 cup quick-cooking whole-grain brown rice
- 1+1/2 cups lower-sodium chicken broth
- 2 roasted red peppers (from a jar), thinly sliced
- Pinch saffron
- 1/2 pound large shrimp, peeled and deveined
- 2 large plum tomatoes, chopped
- 1/2 cup fresh or frozen baby peas
- 1+1/2 pounds littleneck clams or cockles (about 2 dozen), cleaned
- 1+1/2 pounds mussels (about 2 dozen), cleaned
- Freshly ground black pepper

DIRECTION

1. In a large saucepan, heat oil over medium heat. Add sausage and cook until browned on all sides, about 5 minutes; transfer to a cutting board. Add onion and garlic to the pan; cook over medium heat until softened, about 5 minutes.
2. Meanwhile, cut sausage into thin slices. Return sausage to the pan and add wine, scraping up any browned bits from the bottom of the pan. Add rice, broth, red peppers, and saffron; bring to a simmer, cover, and cook for 5 minutes. Stir in shrimp, tomatoes, and peas.
3. Add clams and mussels, cover, and cook until clams and mussels open, about 5 minutes. Discard any shellfish that haven't opened. Season lightly with black pepper. Divide among 4 bowls and serve warm.

CRAB AND SHRIMP CAKES WITH CAPER SAUCE

 Prep: 25 min
 Cooking: 25 min
 Serve: 4

NUTRITION:
Per serving: 270 calories, 12 g fat, 2 g saturated fat, 36 g protein, 3 g carbohydrate, 0 g fiber, 700 mg sodium

INGREDIENTS

Sauce
- 2 tablespoons capers, rinsed and drained
- 2 tablespoons mayonnaise
- 1 tablespoon fresh lemon juice
- 1/2 teaspoon Dijon mustard

Cakes
- 3 teaspoons extra-virgin olive oil
- 1/2 pound large shrimp, peeled and deveined
- 1 medium yellow or red bell pepper, finely chopped
- 2 medium shallots, finely chopped
- 1 pound fresh lump crabmeat
- 1 large egg
- 2 tablespoons finely chopped chives
- 1 teaspoon Dijon mustard

DIRECTION

1. For the sauce: In a food processor, combine capers, mayonnaise, lemon juice, and mustard; pulse until capers are very finely chopped. Transfer to an airtight container and refrigerate until ready to use. For the cakes: In a large nonstick skillet, heat 1+1/2 teaspoons of the oil over high heat. Add shrimp and cook until pink, about 1 minute per side; transfer to a plate to cool.
2. Add pepper and shallots to the skillet and reduce the heat to medium; cook, stirring frequently, until just beginning to soften, about 2 minutes. Transfer to a medium bowl. Place cooled shrimp in the food processor and pulse until finely chopped. Add to the bowl with pepper and shallots.
3. Add crab, egg, chives, and mustard to shrimp mixture; stir well. Form mixture into 8 cakes, 1 inch thick. Transfer to a plate, cover with plastic wrap, and refrigerate for 30 minutes. In the same large nonstick skillet, heat remaining 1+1/2 teaspoons oil over medium heat. Add cakes and cook until golden on the outside and warmed through, about 4 minutes per side (turn carefully). Divide among 4 plates and serve warm, topped with caper sauce

GRILLED FISH TACOS WITH SPICY MELON SALSA

 Prep: 15 min

 Cooking: 15 min

 Serve: 4

NUTRITION:

Per serving: 231 calories, 7 g fat, 1 g saturated fat, 23 g protein, 19 g carbohydrate, 3 g fiber, 353 mg sodium

INGREDIENTS

- 3 tablespoons fresh lime juice
- 3 teaspoons extra-virgin olive oil
- 1 pound skinless sea bass fillets
- 1/4 teaspoon salt
- Freshly ground black pepper
- 2 cups finely chopped cantaloupe (about 2+1/2-pound melon)
- 1/4 cup chopped fresh cilantro
- 2 scallions, thinly sliced
- 1 jalapeño, seeded and minced
- 2 (10-inch) whole-wheat tortillas
- 1 lime, cut into wedges

DIRECTION

1. In a 9- by 13-inch glass baking dish, whisk together 1 tablespoon of the lime juice and 1 teaspoon of the oil. Add fish and turn to coat. Sprinkle with salt and season lightly with black pepper. Lightly coat a grill or grill pan with cooking spray and heat to medium-high.
2. Grill fish until opaque and tender, about 5 minutes per side. Transfer fish to a cutting board and cut into 1-inch chunks. In a small bowl, combine cantaloupe, cilantro, scallions, jalapeño, remaining 2 tablespoons lime juice, and remaining 2 teaspoons oil.
3. Grill tortillas until warm, about 30 seconds per side. Cut each into 4 quarters. Divide fish among tortillas, top with melon salsa, and serve warm with lime wedges

WARM SHRIMP AND PENNE WITH DILL

 Prep: 20 min

 Cooking: 30 min

 Serve: 4

NUTRITION:

Per serving: 330 calories, 3.5 g fat, 0 g saturated fat, 28 g protein, 46 g carbohydrate, 6 g fiber, 370 mg sodium

INGREDIENTS

- 1 pound large shrimp, peeled and deveined
- 8 ounces whole-wheat penne
- 1 cup grape tomatoes, halved
- 1/2 cup low-fat or nonfat plain yogurt
- 3 scallions, finely sliced
- 2 tablespoons chopped fresh dill
- 1 tablespoon capers, rinsed, drained, and chopped
- 2 teaspoons finely grated lemon zest
- 1/4 teaspoon salt
- 1/4 teaspoon freshly ground black pepp

DIRECTION

1. Bring a large saucepan of water to a boil. Add shrimp, return to a simmer, and cook until shrimp turn pink, 1 to 2 minutes. Using a slotted spoon, transfer shrimp to a large bowl; keep water boiling over high heat.
2. Add pasta to boiling water and cook according to package directions until al dente.
3. Drain (do not rinse) and add to the bowl with shrimp. Add tomatoes, yogurt, scallions, dill, capers, lemon zest, salt, and pepper to the bowl with pasta and shrimp; toss well. Serve warm.

GRILLED SALMON AND FARRO SALAD

Prep: 10 min   Cooking: 40 min

Serve: 4

NUTRITION:
Per serving: 350 calories, 17 g fat, 3 g saturated fat, 27 g protein, 23 g carbohydrate, 6 g fiber, 220 mg sodium

INGREDIENTS

- 1/2 cup farro
- 1 pound salmon fillet (about 3/4 inch thick), skin removed
- 3 teaspoons extra-virgin olive oil
- Freshly ground black pepper
- 1/4 cup finely chopped fresh parsley
- 3 scallions, thinly sliced
- 1 tablespoon grated orange zest
- 2 teaspoons fresh lemon juice
- 1/4 teaspoon salt
- 4 large red leaf lettuce leaves

DIRECTION

1. Bring a medium saucepan of water to a boil, add farro, and cook until tender, 25 to 30 minutes. Drain (do not rinse) and transfer to a large bowl. While farro is cooking, lightly coat a grill or grill pan with cooking spray and heat to medium-high. Brush salmon with 1 teaspoon of the oil and season lightly with pepper. Grill salmon until it can be flaked with a fork, 4 to 5 minutes per side.
2. Transfer to a cutting board; when cool enough to handle, flake with a fork into the bowl with farro. Add parsley, scallions, orange zest, lemon juice, salt, and remaining 2 teaspoons oil to farro and salmon; toss well. Season with pepper to taste.
3. Divide lettuce among 4 plates, top with farro mixture, and serve warm or at room temperature

SEARED SCALLOPS WITH SUMMER VEGETABLES

Prep: 20 min　　Cooking: 20 min

Serve: 4

NUTRITION:

Per serving with corn: 180 calories, 8 g fat, 1 g saturated fat, 18 g protein, 11 g carbohydrate, 2 g fiber, 280 mg sodium

INGREDIENTS

- 4 teaspoons extra-virgin olive oil
- 1+1/2 pounds sea scallops (about 20), cleaned
- 1/4 teaspoon salt
- Freshly ground black pepper
- 1 medium zucchini, halved lengthwise and thinly sliced into half-moons
- 1/2 small onion, finely chopped
- 2 garlic cloves, minced
- 1 cup cherry tomatoes, halved
- 3/4 cup frozen shelled edamame, defrosted
- 1 small ear of corn, shucked, kernels sliced off cob (1/2 cup kernels)
- 2 tablespoons chopped fresh basil

DIRECTION

1. In a large nonstick skillet, heat 2 teaspoons of the oil over medium-high heat. Add scallops, sprinkle with 1/8 teaspoon of the salt, and season lightly with pepper. Cook until golden brown on the outside and opaque inside, about 2 to 3 minutes per side.
2. Transfer to a plate and keep warm. Reduce the heat to medium and add remaining 2 teaspoons oil to the pan. Add zucchini, onion, and garlic; cook until vegetables are softened, about 5 minutes. Add tomatoes, edamame, and corn; cook until tomatoes begin to break down, 3 to 4 minutes.
3. Return scallops to the pan and sprinkle with remaining 1/8 teaspoon salt and pepper to taste; reheat for 30 seconds, or until heated through. Stir in basil. Divide among 4 plates and serve warm

GRILLED TUNA WITH PROVENÇAL ANCHOVY SAUCE

Prep: 5 min   Cooking: 10 min   Serve: 4

NUTRITION:
Per serving: 220 calories, 5 g fat, 1 g saturated fat, 40 g protein, 0 g carbohydrate, 0 g fiber, 105 mg sodium

INGREDIENTS

- 1+1/2 pounds tuna steaks, about 1+1/4 inches thick
- 1 tablespoon extra-virgin olive oil
- 1 small garlic clove, minced
- 1/2 teaspoon herbes de Provence
- 2 anchovy fillets
- 1 tablespoon red wine vinegar
- 1 tablespoon chopped fresh parsley

DIRECTION

1. Lightly coat a grill or grill pan with cooking spray and heat to medium-high. Grill tuna 2 to 3 minutes per side for medium-rare. Transfer to a cutting board. In a small saucepan, heat oil over medium-low heat.
2. Add garlic and cook, stirring with a wooden spoon, until softened but not browned, about 1 minute. Add herbes de Provence and anchovies, mashing anchovies with the back of the wooden spoon until they break up, about 30 seconds. Remove the pan from the heat and stir in vinegar and parsley.
3. Transfer anchovy sauce to a small bowl. Thinly slice tuna, divide among 4 plates, and drizzle with anchovy sauce. Serve warm.

MIXED SEAFOOD KEBABS WITH PARSLEY-GARLIC SAUCE

Prep: 30 min

Cooking: 20 min

Serve: 4

NUTRITION:
Per serving: 280 calories, 7 g fat, 1 g saturated fat, 44 g protein, 8 g carbohydrate, 1 g fiber, 400 mg sodium

INGREDIENTS

Sauce
- 2 large garlic cloves, minced
- 1+1/2 tablespoons finely chopped fresh parsley
- 1 tablespoon extra-virgin olive oil
- 1 tablespoon fresh lemon juice
- 1/4 teaspoon salt

Kebabs
- 1 pound sea scallops (about 16), cleaned
- 1 pound halibut fillet (about 1+1/4 inches thick), skin removed, fish cut into 1+1/2-inch pieces
- 1 large zucchini, cut into 1/2-inch-thick rounds
- 1 small red onion, cut into 1/2-inch-thick wedges
- 1/4 teaspoon freshly ground black pepper

Special equipment
- 8 (12-inch) skewers

DIRECTION

1. For the sauce: Place garlic in a small saucepan and add water just to cover. Bring to a boil, reduce the heat, and simmer for 5 minutes; strain and transfer garlic to a small bowl. Add parsley, oil, lemon juice, and salt to garlic; stir to combine.
2. For the kebabs: Thread scallops, halibut, zucchini, and onion alternately onto skewers; season with pepper. Generously coat a grill or grill pan with cooking spray and heat to mediumhigh.
3. Grill kebabs, turning once, until fish is cooked through and vegetables are lightly charred, 10 to 12 minutes. Serve warm or at room temperature, drizzled with parsley-garlic sauce.

PASTA WITH SALMON, PEAS, MINT, AND FETA

Prep: 15 min Cooking: 20 min Serve: 4

NUTRITION:
Per serving: 460 calories, 15 g fat, 3.5 g saturated fat, 36 g protein, 49 g carbohydrate, 9 g fiber, 440 mg sodium

INGREDIENTS

- 1 pound salmon fillet (about 1 inch thick), skin removed
- 1 (8-ounce) package shaped whole-wheat pasta
- 1 cup fresh or frozen baby peas
- 2 ounces crumbled reduced-fat feta cheese (1/3 cup)
- 1/4 cup chopped fresh mint, plus mint leaves for garnish
- 2 tablespoons fresh lemon juice
- 1/4 teaspoon salt

DIRECTION

1. Heat the broiler. Cover a broiler pan with foil and lightly coat with cooking spray. Place salmon on the broiler pan and broil until fish is opaque and cooked through, about 10 minutes. Remove salmon from the broiler and transfer to a large bowl. When cool enough to handle, cut into bite-size pieces.
2. While salmon is cooking, bring a large saucepan of lightly salted water to a boil. Cook pasta according to package directions until al dente, adding peas during the last 2 minutes of cooking. Reserving 1/4 cup of the pasta cooking water, drain pasta and peas and transfer to the bowl with salmon.
3. In a medium bowl, whisk together feta, mint, lemon juice, salt, and reserved 1/4 cup pasta cooking water to make a sauce. Pour sauce over pasta and salmon and toss gently to coat. Serve warm.

SPICY BBQ SHRIMP AND RICE

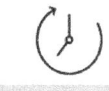
Prep: 25 min

Cooking: 20 min

Serve: 4

NUTRITION:
Per serving: 370 calories, 12 g fat, 2 g saturated fat, 43 g protein, 22 g carbohydrate, 3 g fiber, 580 mg sodium

INGREDIENTS

Rice
- 1 tablespoon extra-virgin olive oil
- 3 scallions, white and green parts thinly sliced and kept separate
- 1 medium green bell pepper, finely chopped
- 1 cup quick-cooking whole-grain brown rice
- 1+3/4 cups water

Shrimp
- 1 tablespoon extra-virgin olive oil
- 1 tablespoon paprika
- 1 teaspoon garlic powder
- 1/2 teaspoon dried thyme
- 4 scallions, thinly sliced
- 1 tablespoon fresh lemon juice
- 1 tablespoon Worcestershire sauce
- 3/4 cup tomato sauce
- 2 tablespoons granular sugar substitute
- 2 teaspoons hot pepper sauce
- 2 pounds large shrimp, peeled and deveined

DIRECTION

1. For the rice: In a large nonstick saucepan, heat oil over medium heat. Add scallion whites and pepper; cook, stirring, until vegetables just begin to soften, about 5 minutes. Add rice and stir to coat. Add water, cover, and cook rice according to package directions.
2. For the shrimp: While rice is cooking, in a large nonstick skillet heat oil over medium heat. Add paprika, garlic powder, and thyme; cook, stirring, until fragrant, about 1 minute. Stir in scallions, lemon juice, Worcestershire sauce, tomato sauce, sugar substitute, and hot pepper sauce; cook 1 minute more.
3. Add shrimp and toss to coat with sauce; cover and cook 2 to 3 minutes, or until shrimp turn pink. Remove from the heat and keep warm. To serve, divide rice among 4 plates, top with shrimp, and sprinkle with scallion greens

LEMON-GRILLED WHOLE TROUT WITH PESTO

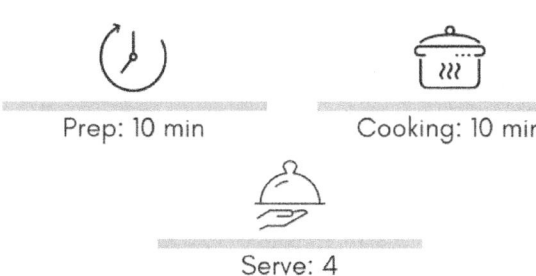

Prep: 10 min   Cooking: 10 min   Serve: 4

NUTRITION:
Per serving: 280 calories, 13 g fat, 2.5 g saturated fat, 36 g protein, 1 g carbohydrate, 0 g fiber, 260 mg sodium

INGREDIENTS

- 4 whole trout (about 12 ounces each), cleaned and boned
- 1 tablespoon extra-virgin olive oil
- 1/4 teaspoon salt
- Freshly ground black pepper
- 3 lemons
- 2 tablespoons store-bought pesto

DIRECTION

1. Lightly coat the outside of each trout with oil. Sprinkle evenly inside and out with salt and season lightly with pepper. Slice 2 of the lemons into 8 slices each. Place 4 slices, slightly overlapping, inside the cavity of each fish.
2. Cut remaining lemon into wedges. Lightly coat a grill or grill pan with cooking spray and heat to medium-high. Grill fish until lightly browned on the outside and opaque and tender inside, about 5 minutes per side. Remove from the grill and remove heads and tails, if desired.
3. Remove and discard lemon slices. Place fish on 4 serving plates, gently open each, flesh side up, and spread 1+1/2 teaspoons pesto on the inside of each fish. Serve warm with lemon wedges.

STEAMED MUSSELS WITH GARDEN VEGETABLE BROTH

 Prep: 20 min

 Cooking: 10 min

 Serve: 4

NUTRITION:
Per serving: 190 calories, 7 g fat, 1 g saturated fat, 18 g protein, 10 g carbohydrate, 2 g fiber, 400 mg sodium

INGREDIENTS

- 1 tablespoon extra-virgin olive oil
- 1 medium zucchini, cut into 1/2-inch pieces
- 2 scallions, white and green parts thinly sliced and kept separate
- 2 medium plum tomatoes, cut into 1/2-inch cubes
- 1/3 cup white wine
- 2 garlic cloves, minced
- 4 pounds mussels, cleaned
- 2 tablespoons thinly sliced fresh basil

DIRECTION

1. In a large nonstick saucepan, heat oil over medium-high heat. Add zucchini and scallion whites; cook, stirring, until zucchini begins to brown, about 3 minutes.
2. Stir in tomatoes, wine, and garlic; bring to a simmer.
3. Add mussels, stir, and cover. Steam mussels until they open, about 5 minutes, gently stirring halfway through cooking. Discard any mussels that haven't opened. Divide mussels, broth, and vegetables among 4 bowls. Sprinkle with scallion greens and basil; serve hot.

ASIAN TUNA BURGERS

Prep: 10 min　Cooking: 10 min　Serve: 4

NUTRITION:
Per serving with bun: 330 calories, 12 g fat, 3 g saturated fat, 31 g protein, 24 g carbohydrate, 4 g fiber, 440 mg sodium

INGREDIENTS

- 1 tablespoon sesame seeds
- 1 pound fresh tuna, cut into 1-inch chunks
- 2 scallions, coarsely chopped
- 1 tablespoon Dijon mustard
- 2 teaspoons toasted sesame oil
- 1+1/2 teaspoons low-sodium soy sauce
- 2 tablespoons reduced-fat sour cream
- 1/2 teaspoon fresh lemon juice
- 1/4 teaspoon wasabi paste
- 4 whole-wheat or whole-grain buns, lightly toasted (optional)

DIRECTION

1. In a small skillet, toast sesame seeds over medium-low heat, shaking the pan back and forth until seeds are golden, about 5 minutes. Transfer to a plate to cool.
2. In a food processor, combine tuna, scallions, mustard, sesame oil, soy sauce, and sesame seeds. Pulse just until mixture comes together (it should not be finely ground), 15 to 20 seconds. Form mixture into 4 patties, about 3/4 inch thick.
3. In a small bowl, whisk together sour cream, lemon juice, and wasabi.
4. Lightly coat a grill or grill pan with cooking spray and heat to medium-high. Grill patties 2 to 3 minutes per side for medium-rare. Place burgers on buns, if using; top each burger with wasabi sauce and serve.

SOUTH-OF-THE-BORDER SALMON BURGERS

Prep: 15 min Cooking: 12 min Serve: 4

NUTRITION:
Per serving: 330 calories, 23 g fat, 5 g saturated fat, 25 g protein, 6 g carbohydrate, 3 g fiber, 260 mg sodium

INGREDIENTS

- 1 pound salmon fillet, skin removed, fish cut into 1-inch chunks
- 2 teaspoons plus 1
- /4 cup reduced-fat sour cream
- 1+1/2 teaspoons Dijon mustard
- 1 teaspoon chili powder
- 1/2 teaspoon ground cumin
- 1/4 teaspoon salt
- Freshly ground black pepper
- 1 (8-ounce) head romaine, shredded (4 cups)
- 1 medium avocado, cubed
- 2 teaspoons extra-virgin olive oil
- 2 teaspoons fresh lime juice
- 1 tablespoon chopped fresh cilantro
- 1/2 teaspoon cayenne

DIRECTION

1. In a food processor, combine salmon, 2 teaspoons of the sour cream, mustard, chili powder, cumin, 1/8 teaspoon of the salt, and 1/8 teaspoon black pepper; pulse just until mixture comes together, 15 to 20 seconds. Form mixture into 4 patties, about 3/4 inch thick.
2. Lightly coat a grill or grill pan with cooking spray and heat to medium-high. Grill patties until cooked through, 4 to 5 minutes per side. While patties are cooking, in a large bowl combine lettuce, avocado, oil, 1 teaspoon of the lime juice, and remaining 1/8 teaspoon salt. Season with black pepper to taste.
3. In a small bowl, whisk together remaining 1/4 cup sour cream, remaining 1 teaspoon lime juice, cilantro, and cayenne. Divide salad among 4 plates and place a burger alongside. Top each burger with a dollop of cilantro sour cream and serve.

TROPICAL SHRIMP AND RICE

 Prep: 20 min

 Cooking: 15 min

 Serve: 4

NUTRITION:

Per serving: 230 calories, 10 g fat, 4 g saturated fat, 21 g protein, 15 g carbohydrate, 2 g fiber, 300 mg sodium

INGREDIENTS

- 1/2 cup quick-cooking whole-grain brown rice
- 1/4 cup unsweetened shredded coconut
- 1 pound large shrimp, peeled and deveined
- 1 small mango, peeled and cut into 1/2-inch cubes
- 1/4 cup chopped fresh parsley
- 1 tablespoon extra-virgin olive oil
- 1 teaspoon grated lime zest
- 1 tablespoon fresh lime juice
- 1/4 teaspoon salt
- 1/8 teaspoon freshly ground black pepper

DIRECTION

1. Cook rice according to package directions. Transfer to a large bowl to cool. While rice is cooking, heat the oven to 350°F.
2. Spread coconut on a baking sheet and bake until golden, about 5 minutes. Transfer to a plate to cool. Bring a saucepan of lightly salted water to a boil. Add shrimp, reduce to a simmer, and cook until shrimp turn pink, 1 to 2 minutes.
3. Transfer shrimp to the bowl with rice. Add coconut, mango, parsley, oil, lime zest, lime juice, salt, and pepper to shrimp mixture; toss well.
4. Divide shrimp and rice among 4 bowls and serve at room temperature

GRILLED SPANISH MACKEREL WITH QUICK PICKLED ONIONS

Prep: 15 min

Cooking: 25 min

Serve: 4

NUTRITION:
Per serving: 250 calories, 11 g fat, 3 g saturated fat, 33 g protein, 4 g carbohydrate, 0 g fiber, 250 mg sodium

INGREDIENTS

- 1 medium red onion, thinly sliced
- 1/4 cup red wine vinegar
- 1 garlic clove, thinly sliced
- 2 teaspoons granular sugar substitute Salt
- Freshly ground black pepper
- 4 (6-ounce) Spanish mackerel fillets, with skin
- 1 tablespoon fresh lemon juice
- 1+1/2 teaspoons grated lemon zest
- 1/2 teaspoon dried oregano

DIRECTION

1. In a small saucepan, combine onion, vinegar, garlic, sugar substitute, salt, and pepper; bring to a simmer, stirring occasionally, and cook until onions are softened and translucent, about 10 minutes. Transfer onions to a serving bowl. Lightly coat a grill or grill pan with cooking spray and heat to medium-high.
2. Drizzle flesh side of fish evenly with lemon juice and sprinkle with lemon zest and oregano. Lightly season with salt and pepper.
3. Grill fish, skin side down, for 5 minutes; turn and grill 5 to 7 minutes more, or until fish is cooked through and tender.
4. Divide fish among 4 plates and serve hot with pickled onions on top or on the side.

NEW ENGLAND SHELLFISH CHOWDER

Prep: 20 min

Cooking: 30 min

Serve: 6

NUTRITION:
Per serving: 300 calories, 6 g fat, 1.5 g saturated fat, 39 g protein, 21 g carbohydrate, 2 g fiber, 630 mg sodium

INGREDIENTS

- 1 tablespoon extra-virgin olive oil
- 1 large onion, finely chopped
- 2 celery stalks, finely chopped
- 3 ounces Canadian bacon, cut into 1/4-inch cubes
- 1 medium sweet potato (8 ounces), peeled and cut into 1/2-inch cubes
- 2 (8-ounce) bottles clam juice
- 2 (6+1/2-ounce) cans chopped clams, with liquid
- 3/4 pound bay scallops or chopped sea scallops
- 1/2 pound shrimp, peeled, deveined, and chopped
- 1+1/2 cups 1% milk
- Freshly ground black pepper

DIRECTION

1. In a large nonstick saucepan, heat oil over medium heat. Add onion and celery, cover, and cook until softened, 3 to 5 minutes. Add bacon and cook until lightly browned, about 5 minutes. Add sweet potato and clam juice; bring to a simmer, partially cover, and cook until sweet potato has softened, about 10 minutes.
2. Stir in clams and their liquid, scallops, shrimp, and milk; return to a simmer and cook, uncovered, until shrimp are pink and scallops are opaque and tender, 3 to 5 minutes. Season lightly with pepper. Divide among 6 bowls and serve hot.

GRILLED SHRIMP SALAD WITH CHILE-LIME DRESSING

Prep: 40 min

Cooking: 10 min

Serve: 4

NUTRITION:
Per serving with papaya: 369 calories, 21.5 g fat, 3 g saturated fat, 26 g protein, 19 g carbohydrate, 7 g fiber, 265 mg sodium

INGREDIENTS

Shrimp
- 1+1/2 tablespoons extra-virgin olive oil
- 2 teaspoons minced garlic
- 1/4 teaspoon crushed red pepper flakes
- 12 to 16 jumbo shrimp (1 to 1 /2 pounds), peeled and deveined, tails left on
- 4 to 6 scallions, each cut into two (2-inch) pieces

Salad
- 2 tablespoons fresh lime juice
- 2 tablespoons extra-virgin olive oil
- 2 small jalapenos, seeded and minced
- 1/4 teaspoon freshly ground black pepper
- **Salt**
- 4 cups mixed greens, such as frisee, mizuna, radish shoots, and radicchio
- 1 medium papaya, seeded and diced
- 1 medium avocado, thinly sliced
- 1 medium red bell pepper, diced
- Special equipment
- 4 (12-inch) skewers

DIRECTION

1. For the shrimp: In a medium bowl, whisk together oil, garlic, and red pepper flakes. Add shrimp and scallions and toss to coat; refrigerate for 30 minutes. For the salad: In a small bowl, whisk together lime juice, oil, jalapeños, black pepper, and 1 /8 teaspoon salt; let stand at room temperature while shrimp is marinating. In a large bowl, combine greens, papaya, avocado, and bell pepper. Generously coat a grill or grill pan with cooking spray and heat to mediumhigh.
2. Alternately thread shrimp and scallions onto 4 skewers. Lightly sprinkle shrimp and scallions with salt and grill, turning once and basting with any remaining marinade, until shrimp just turn pink, 2 to 3 minutes per side. Remove shrimp and scallions from skewers and add to salad mixture.
3. Add dressing and toss gently. Arrange salad on 4 plates and serve.

PROVENÇAL BOUILLABAISSE

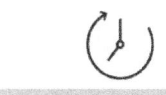
Prep: 25 min

Cooking: 25 min

Serve: 4

NUTRITION:
Per serving: 210 calories, 5 g fat, 1 g saturated fat, 28 g protein, 10 g carbohydrate, 2 g fiber, 560 mg sodium

INGREDIENTS

- 1 tablespoon extra-virgin olive oil
- 1 small fennel bulb, finely chopped, fronds finely chopped for garnish
- 1 small leek, white part only, finely chopped
- 2 garlic cloves, smashed and peeled
- 1/4 teaspoon dried thyme
- 1/4 cup white wine
- 2 large plum tomatoes, chopped
- 3 cups lower-sodium chicken broth Pinch saffron
- 1 pound cod or haddock fillets, skin removed, fish cut into 2-inch pieces
- 1/2 pound mussels (about 8), cleaned
- 1/2 pound littleneck clams or cockles (about 8), scrubbed

DIRECTION

1. In a large nonstick saucepan, heat oil over medium heat. Add fennel bulb, leek, garlic, and thyme; cover, reduce heat to medium-low, and cook until vegetables are softened, about 5 minutes. Stir in wine and tomatoes; cook, uncovered, until liquid has almost evaporated, about 1 minute. Add broth and saffron; bring to a simmer. Add cod, cover, and cook for 5 minutes.
2. Add mussels and clams, cover, and cook until shells are opened, about 5 minutes more. Discard any shellfish that haven't opened. Ladle bouillabaisse into 4 large bowls, sprinkle with chopped fennel fronds, and serve hot.

CHAPTER 5
EASY SUMMER POULTRY

GRILLED CHICKEN WITH SAVORY ASIAN PLUM SAUCE

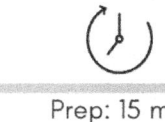 Prep: 15 min

 Cooking: 30 min

 Serve: 4

NUTRITION:
Per serving: 285 calories, 6 g fat, 1 g saturated fat, 40 g protein, 15 g carbohydrate, 2 g fiber, 260 mg sodium

INGREDIENTS

- 4 (6-ounce) boneless, skinless chicken breasts
- 1 tablespoon fresh lime juice
- 3 garlic cloves, minced
- 2 teaspoons extra-virgin olive oil
- 1 teaspoon toasted sesame oil
- 6 medium plums, cut into eighths
- 2 tablespoons mirin
- 2 teaspoons finely grated lime zest
- 1 teaspoon grated fresh ginger
- 1/4 teaspoon salt
- Freshly ground black pepper
- Fresh herbs, greens, or sprouts for garnish

DIRECTION

1. In a resealable plastic bag, combine chicken, lime juice, garlic, and olive oil; turn to coat. Marinate chicken at room temperature for 15 minutes or refrigerate overnight.
2. In a medium nonstick skillet, heat sesame oil over medium heat. Add plums, mirin, lime zest, ginger, salt, and pepper to taste. Cook, stirring gently, until plums are softened, 10 to 15 minutes, depending on ripeness (do not allow plums to completely lose their shape). Remove the pan from the heat, cover, and keep warm.
3. Lightly coat a grill or grill pan with cooking spray and heat to medium-high. Remove chicken from marinade and grill until cooked through, 5 to 7 minutes per side. Discard any remaining marinade. Divide chicken among 4 plates and serve warm, topped with plum sauce. Garnish as desired.

GARLICKY CHICKEN SKEWERS

Prep: 15 min   Cooking: 10 min

Serve: 4

NUTRITION:
Per serving: 260 calories, 6 g fat, 1 g saturated fat, 42 g protein, 11 g carbohydrate, 5 g fiber, 270 mg sodium

INGREDIENTS

- 1+1/2 pounds boneless, skinless chicken breasts, cut into 1-inch pieces
- 3 garlic cloves, finely minced
- 2 teaspoons dried rosemary
- 3 teaspoons extra-virgin olive oil
- Salt
- Freshly ground black pepper
- 1 small eggplant (1 pound), peeled and cut into 1/2-inch cubes
- 3 small zucchini, cut into 1 /2-inch-thick rounds

Special equipment
- 8 (12-inch) skewers

DIRECTION

1. Lightly coat a grill or grill pan with cooking spray and heat to medium-high. In a medium bowl, combine chicken, garlic, rosemary, 2 teaspoons of the oil, 1 /4 teaspoon salt, and 1 /8 teaspoon pepper; stir to coat well.
2. Thread equal amounts of chicken onto 4 skewers. In the same bowl, toss eggplant and zucchini pieces with remaining 1 teaspoon oil. Thread eggplant and zucchini pieces evenly onto 4 remaining skewers. Lightly season with salt and pepper.
3. Grill chicken and vegetable skewers, turning every 2 minutes, until chicken is cooked through and vegetables are tender and lightly browned, about 8 minutes for chicken and 10 minutes for vegetables. Serve warm.

PULLED TURKEY SANDWICHES

Prep: 5 min

Cooking: 50 min

Serve: 4

NUTRITION:
Per serving with bun: 350 calories, 4 g fat, 0.5 g saturated fat, 48 g protein, 30 g carbohydrate, 4 g fiber, 590 mg sodium

INGREDIENTS

- 1 (14-ounce) can lower-sodium chicken broth
- 1 (8-ounce) can no-salt-added tomato sauce
- 2 tablespoons apple cider vinegar
- 2 tablespoons sugar-free pancake syrup
- 3 garlic cloves, minced
- 1 tablespoon Worcestershire sauce
- 2 teaspoons mustard powder
- 1 teaspoon red pepper flakes
- 1+1/2 pounds boneless, skinless turkey breast, cut into 4 or 5 pieces
- 4 whole-wheat or whole-grain hamburger buns (optional)

DIRECTION

1. In a medium saucepan, combine broth, tomato sauce, vinegar, syrup, garlic, Worcestershire sauce, mustard, and pepper flakes; bring to a boil over mediumhigh heat.
2. Reduce the heat to low and add turkey; cover and simmer for 30 minutes. Using a slotted spoon, transfer turkey to a large bowl to cool for about 10 minutes. Continue cooking sauce, uncovered, until reduced by half, 10 to 15 minutes (you should have at least 1 cup). Remove from the heat and transfer 1/2 cup of the sauce to a small bowl, leaving remaining sauce in the pan.
3. Using 2 forks, shred (pull) turkey. Return pulled turkey to the saucepan and stir to coat evenly with remaining sauce. Cook over low heat just to warm through, about 3 minutes. Divide turkey meat among buns, if using, and drizzle evenly with reserved sauce. Serve warm.

MEDITERRANEAN CHICKEN BURGERS

 Prep: 15 min

 Cooking: 10 min

 Serve: 4

NUTRITION:
Per serving with bun: 340 calories, 8 g fat, 1.5 g saturated fat, 34 g protein, 36 g carbohydrate, 7 g fiber, 830 mg sodium

INGREDIENTS

- 1 (13+3/4-ounce) can quartered artichoke hearts in water, drained
- 1/4 cup sun-dried tomatoes in oil (about 6), cut into thin strips
- 1 pound ground chicken breast
- 1 large egg yolk
- 1 tablespoon Dijon mustard
- 2 teaspoons Worcestershire sauce
- 1 garlic clove, minced
- 2 tablespoons chopped fresh basil, plus 12 whole basil leaves
- 4 whole-wheat or whole-grain hamburger buns, lightly toasted (optional)

DIRECTION

1. In a small bowl, combine artichoke hearts and tomatoes. In a large bowl, stir together chicken, egg yolk, mustard, Worcestershire sauce, garlic, and chopped basil. Form mixture into 4 patties, about 1/2 inch thick.
2. Lightly coat a large nonstick skillet with cooking spray and heat over medium-high heat.
3. Add burgers and cook until cooked through, about 5 minutes per side. Place basil leaves on buns, if using, and top with burgers. Top each burger with artichoke mixture and serve.

JALAPEÑO TURKEY BURGERS

Prep: 10 min   Cooking: 12 min   Serve: 4

NUTRITION:
Per serving with bun: 301 calories, 8 g fat, 2.5 g saturated fat, 36 g protein, 26 g carbohydrate, 4 g fiber, 500 mg sodium

INGREDIENTS

- 1 pound ground turkey breast
- 1 large egg yolk
- 1 small jalapeño, seeded and chopped
- 3 garlic cloves, minced
- 2 teaspoons Worcestershire sauce
- 2 tablespoons tomato paste
- 2 ounces shredded reduced-fat Monterey Jack cheese (1/2 cup)
- 4 whole-wheat or whole-grain hamburger buns, lightly toasted (optional)

DIRECTION

1. In a large bowl, stir together turkey, egg yolk, jalapeño, garlic, Worcestershire sauce, and tomato paste. Form mixture into 4 patties, about 3/4 inch thick. Lightly coat a large nonstick skillet with cooking spray and heat over medium-high heat.
2. Add burgers and cook until cooked through, about 5 minutes per side. Top each burger with cheese and cook until cheese melts, about 1 minute more. Serve on buns, if using

QUICK CHICKEN TAGINE

 Prep: 25 min

 Cooking: 25 min

Serve: 4

NUTRITION:
Per serving: 310 calories, 10 g fat, 1 g saturated fat, 42 g protein, 13 g carbohydrate, 4 g fiber, 380 mg sodium

INGREDIENTS

- 2 garlic cloves
- 2 (3-inch) pieces lemon zest
- 3 tablespoons chopped fresh parsley, plus leaves for garnish
- 1/2 teaspoon ground coriander
- 1/2 teaspoon ground cumin
- 1/4 teaspoon ground cinnamon
- Freshly ground black pepper
- 1 tablespoon extra-virgin olive oil
- 1+1/2 pounds boneless, skinless chicken breasts, cut into 1-inch cubes
- 1 medium onion, chopped
- 1 (14-ounce) can no-salt-added diced tomatoes, with juices
- 3 tablespoons fresh lemon juice
- 2 medium zucchini, cut into 1/2-inch cubes
- 20 pitted medium green olives, halved
- Pinch salt

DIRECTION

1. On a cutting board, finely chop 1 clove of the garlic together with 1 piece of the lemon zest and 1 tablespoon of the parsley to make a rough paste; transfer to a small bowl and set aside. Mince remaining garlic clove and place in another small bowl; mix in coriander, cumin, cinnamon, and pepper.
2. In a large nonstick skillet, heat oil over medium-high heat. Add chicken and cook, turning occasionally, until lightly browned, 3 to 4 minutes. Transfer chicken to a plate.
3. Reduce the heat under the skillet to medium and add onion and spice mixture; cook, stirring constantly, until onion is softened and spices are aromatic, 2 to 3 minutes. Add tomatoes and their juices and lemon juice, scraping up any brown bits clinging to the skillet; bring to a simmer. Return chicken pieces and their juices to the skillet and cook for 5 minutes. Add zucchini, olives, remaining lemon zest, and remaining 2 tablespoons parsley; stir gently to combine. Reduce the heat to low, cover, and cook until chicken is cooked through, 10 minutes more. Lightly season with salt and pepper. Divide tagine among 4 bowls, top with reserved parsley paste, and garnish with parsley leaves.

CURRIED CHICKEN SALAD WITH PEANUTS

Prep: 15 min

Cooking: 15 min

Serve: 4

NUTRITION:
Per serving: 440 calories, 22 g fat, 3.5 g saturated fat, 47 g protein, 15 g carbohydrate, 4 g fiber, 410 mg sodium

INGREDIENTS

- 2 teaspoons extra-virgin olive oil
- 1+1/2 pounds boneless, skinless chicken breasts
- 2 tablespoons fresh lemon juice
- 12 ounces snow peas, trimmed and cut into 1/2-inch pieces
- 1/2 cup nonfat or low-fat plain yogurt
- 1/4 cup mayonnaise
- 1 tablespoon curry powder
- 2 teaspoons Dijon mustard
- 1 teaspoon finely grated lemon zest
- 1/4 teaspoon salt
- 2 celery stalks, finely chopped
- 1 small bunch scallions, chopped
- Freshly ground black pepper
- 1/3 cup unsalted roasted peanuts, chopped

DIRECTION

1. In a large nonstick skillet, heat oil over medium-high heat. Add chicken and 1 tablespoon of the lemon juice; cook until chicken is cooked through, 5 to 6 minutes per side. Transfer chicken to a cutting board and let cool to room temperature. When cool, cut into 1/2-inch cubes.
2. While chicken is cooking, bring a medium saucepan of lightly salted water to a boil. Add snow peas and cook for 1 minute. Drain snow peas in a colander and immediately run under very cold water for 1 minute to stop cooking. Drain again and pat dry.
3. In a large bowl, whisk together yogurt, mayonnaise, curry powder, mustard, lemon zest, salt, and remaining 1 tablespoon lemon juice. Add chicken, snow peas, celery, and scallions to yogurt mixture and toss to combine; season with pepper to taste. Divide chicken salad among 4 plates, sprinkle with peanuts, and serve

SPICY CHICKEN AND BLACK BEAN TACOS

Prep: 15 min

Cooking: 15 min

Serve: 4

NUTRITION:
Per serving: 410 calories, 10 g fat, 1 g saturated fat, 36 g protein, 42 g carbohydrate, 8 g fiber, 540 mg sodium

INGREDIENTS

Rub
- 2 teaspoons garlic powder
- 2 teaspoons paprika
- 2 teaspoons dried thyme
- 1 teaspoon cayenne
- 1 teaspoon freshly ground black pepper

Chicken
- 1 pound boneless, skinless chicken breasts
- 1+1/2 tablespoons extra-virgin olive oil
- 1 medium onion, chopped
- 1 (15-ounce) can black beans, rinsed and drained
- 1 medium tomato, chopped
- 1/4 cup minced fresh cilantro, plus whole leaves for garnish
- 4 (8-inch) whole-wheat tortillas

DIRECTION

1. For the rub: In a small bowl, combine garlic powder, paprika, thyme, cayenne, and black pepper.
2. For the chicken: Lightly pound each chicken breast to an even 1/2-inch thickness. Rub a thick layer of the spice mixture onto both sides of each chicken breast. In a large heavy skillet, heat 1 tablespoon of the oil over high heat until hot but not smoking. Add chicken and cook until blackened on both sides and cooked through, 2 to 3 minutes per side. Transfer chicken to a cutting board. Reduce heat to medium and add remaining 1/2 tablespoon oil and onion to the skillet.
3. Cook, stirring to scrape up any brown bits clinging to the bottom of the skillet, until onion is softened, 1 to 2 minutes. Add beans and cook until heated through, 2 to 3 minutes.
4. Remove from the heat and stir in tomato and minced cilantro. Warm tortillas according to package directions. Cut chicken on the diagonal into 1/2-inch-thick slices. Place tortillas on 4 plates. Divide chicken and beans among tortillas.
5. Fold tortillas into cones and top with cilantro leaves.

ASIAN TURKEY MEATBALLS IN LETTUCE CUPS

Prep: 15 min   Cooking: 15 min   Serve: 4

NUTRITION:
Per serving: 180 calories, 6 g fat, 0.5 g saturated fat, 30 g protein, 4 g carbohydrate, 0 g fiber, 480 mg sodium

INGREDIENTS

Dressing
- 1 tablespoon Asian fish sauce
- 1 tablespoon rice vinegar
- 1/2 teaspoon toasted sesame oil
- Pinch red pepper flakes

Meatballs
- 1 pound ground turkey breast
- 2 garlic cloves, minced
- 1 tablespoon grated fresh ginger
- 1 tablespoon toasted sesame oil
- 2 teaspoons rice vinegar
- 2 teaspoons low-sodium soy sauce
- 12 large Boston lettuce leaves
- 1 small cucumber, cut into matchsticks
- 1 cup mint leaves

DIRECTION

1. For the dressing: In a small bowl, whisk together fish sauce, vinegar, sesame oil, and pepper flakes; set aside at room temperature.
2. For the meatballs: In a large bowl, stir together turkey, garlic, ginger, sesame oil, vinegar, and soy sauce. Form mixture into 24 (2-inch) meatballs. Lightly coat a large nonstick skillet with cooking spray and heat to mediumhigh.
3. Add meatballs in two batches and cook, turning occasionally, until browned on all sides, 5 to 7 minutes for each batch. Lay 3 lettuce leaves on each of 4 plates. Place 2 meatballs on top of each leaf. Top meatballs with cucumber and mint leaves, drizzle with dressing, and serve.

PAN-SEARED CHICKEN WITH ROASTED TOMATILLO SALSA

Prep: 15 min

Cooking: 30 min

Serve: 4

NUTRITION:
Per serving: 260 calories, 7 g fat, 1 g saturated fat, 41 g protein, 9 g carbohydrate, 2 g fiber, 115 mg sodium

INGREDIENTS

- 12 ounces fresh tomatillos
- 3 teaspoons extra-virgin olive oil
- 1 medium onion, chopped
- 2 garlic cloves, chopped
- 1/2 cup cilantro leaves
- 1 small jalapeño, seeded and minced
- 1 tablespoon fresh lime juice
- 4 (6-ounce) boneless, skinless chicken breasts
- Salt and freshly ground black pepper

DIRECTION

1. Remove and discard papery skin from tomatillos; rinse and pat dry. Heat the broiler. Place tomatillos on a foil-lined broiler pan; broil for 8 to 10 minutes, turning halfway through, until softened and blackened on all sides.
2. Transfer tomatillos and their juices to a blender or food processor. In a medium nonstick skillet, heat 2 teaspoons of the oil over medium heat. Add onion and garlic; cook, stirring occasionally, until softened and lightly browned, about 5 minutes. Transfer to the blender or food processor with the tomatillos and add cilantro, jalapeño, and lime juice. Pulse for 1 minute, until ingredients form a rough purée. Lightly pound each chicken breast to an even 1/2-inch thickness; season lightly with salt and black pepper.
3. In a large heavy skillet, heat remaining 1 teaspoon oil over high heat until hot but not smoking. Add chicken breasts, reduce the heat to medium-high, and cook until lightly browned and cooked through, 4 to 5 minutes per side. Transfer chicken to a cutting board. Transfer tomatillo salsa to the hot skillet and cook over medium-high heat, stirring constantly, for about 1 minute, until salsa has a darker, thicker color and texture.
4. Remove from the heat. Slice chicken breasts on the diagonal into 1/2-inch-thick slices. Place 1/4 cup of the salsa on each of 4 plates, arrange chicken slices on top, and top with additional salsa. Serve warm.

TURKEY CUTLETS WITH VEGETABLE COUSCOUS

Prep: 20 min

Cooking: 8 min

Serve: 4

NUTRITION:
Per serving: 310 calories, 7 g fat, 1 g saturated fat, 45 g protein, 16 g carbohydrate, 3 g fiber, 300 mg sodium

INGREDIENTS

- 1+1/2 pounds turkey cutlets
- 3 garlic cloves, minced
- 3 tablespoons chopped fresh parsley
- 1 tablespoon plus 2 teaspoons extra-virgin olive oil
- 2 teaspoons finely grated lemon zest
- 1/8 teaspoon red pepper flakes
- 1 small yellow bell pepper, finely chopped
- 1 cup cherry tomatoes, halved
- 1 small cucumber, peeled and cut into 1/4-inch cubes
- 1 tablespoon minced red onion
- 1 tablespoon red wine vinegar
- 1/4 teaspoon salt
- 1/2 cup whole-wheat couscous

DIRECTION

1. In a resealable plastic bag, combine turkey, garlic, parsley, 1 tablespoon of the oil, lemon zest, and pepper flakes; turn to coat well.
2. Marinate at room temperature for 15 minutes or refrigerate overnight. While turkey is marinating, in a large bowl combine remaining 2 teaspoons oil, bell pepper, tomatoes, cucumber, onion, vinegar, and salt. Prepare couscous according to package directions.
3. Add hot couscous to vegetable mixture and stir well; keep warm.
4. Lightly coat a nonstick skillet with cooking spray and heat over mediumhigh heat. Add turkey and marinade to the skillet and cook until cooked through, about 2 minutes per side. Serve warm with vegetable couscous.

GRILLED CHICKEN FAJITAS

 Prep: 15 min

 Cooking: 25 min

 Serve: 4

NUTRITION:
Per serving: 310 calories, 7 g fat, 1 g saturated fat, 45 g protein, 16 g carbohydrate, 3 g fiber, 300 mg sodium

INGREDIENTS

- 1+1/2 pounds boneless, skinless chicken breasts
- 2 tablespoons fresh lime juice
- 3 garlic cloves, minced
- 1/2 small jalapeño, seeded and minced
- Salt and freshly ground black pepper
- 1 large red bell pepper, quartered
- 1 large green bell pepper, quartered
- 1 large red onion, cut into 1/2-inch-thick rounds
- 2 teaspoons extra-virgin olive oil
- 4 (8-inch) whole-wheat tortillas

DIRECTION

1. In a resealable plastic bag, combine chicken, lime juice, garlic, and jalapeño; turn to coat well. Marinate chicken at room temperature for 20 minutes or refrigerate overnight.
2. Remove chicken from marinade and season lightly with salt and black pepper. Lightly coat a grill or grill pan with cooking spray and heat to medium-high. Grill chicken until cooked through, about 5 minutes per side.
3. Transfer to a cutting board. While chicken is cooking, in a medium bowl toss bell peppers and onion with oil. Using a grill basket or grill topper, if necessary, grill vegetables, turning occasionally, until softened and lightly charred, 15 to 20 minutes. Transfer onions to a platter. Transfer peppers to a cutting board and cut into thin strips; transfer to the platter with onions. Grill tortillas until warm and lightly browned, about 30 seconds per side. Wrap in foil to keep warm.
4. Slice chicken breasts into 1/2-inch-thick pieces. Place on the platter with vegetables and serve with warmed tortillas.

JERK CHICKEN WITH COOL ROMAINE SALAD

Prep: 60 min Cooking: 15 min Serve: 4

NUTRITION:
Per serving: 230 calories, 3.5 g fat, 1 g saturated fat, 42 g protein, 8 g carbohydrate, 3 g fiber, 480 mg sodium

INGREDIENTS

- 1+1/2 pounds boneless, skinless chicken breasts
- 1 tablespoon jerk seasoning
- 2 tablespoons reduced-fat sour cream
- 1 tablespoon fresh lime juice
- 1 (1-pound) head romaine lettuce, chopped (8 cups)
- 1 large cucumber, peeled and sliced
- 2 large plum tomatoes, chopped
- 2 scallions, chopped
- 1/4 teaspoon salt

DIRECTION

1. Pound chicken breasts to an even 1/2-inch thickness. Lightly rub jerk seasoning on both sides of chicken breasts. Refrigerate in an airtight container for at least 1 hour
2. Lightly coat a large nonstick skillet with cooking spray and heat over medium-high heat. Add chicken and cook until cooked through, 4 to 5 minutes per side. Transfer to a cutting board, let rest for 5 minutes, then cut into 1/2-inchthick slices.
3. While chicken is resting, in a large bowl combine sour cream and lime juice. Add lettuce, cucumber, tomatoes, scallions, and salt; toss well. Divide salad among 4 plates, top with chicken slices, and serve.

EASY SUMMER CHICKEN CHILI

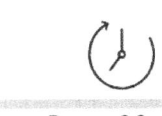
Prep: 20 min

Cooking: 25 min

Serve: 4

NUTRITION:

Per serving: 380 calories, 12 g fat, 2 g saturated fat, 36 g protein, 33 g carbohydrate, 10 g fiber, 560 mg sodium

INGREDIENTS

- 1 small avocado, finely chopped
- 1 tablespoon fresh lime juice
- 1/4 teaspoon salt
- 1 tablespoon extra-virgin olive oil
- 1 medium onion, chopped
- 1 small green bell pepper, chopped
- 1 small zucchini, thinly sliced
- 1 medium jalapeño, seeded and minced
- 1 teaspoon chili powder
- 1/2 teaspoon ground cumin
- 2 cups lower-sodium chicken broth
- 1 (15-ounce) can white beans, rinsed and drained
- 1 (14.5-ounce) can no-salt-added diced tomatoes, with juices
- 1 pound boneless, skinless chicken breasts, cut into 1-inch cubes

DIRECTION

1. In a small bowl, gently stir together avocado, lime juice, and 1/8 teaspoon of the salt.
2. In a large saucepan, heat oil over medium-high heat. Add onion, bell pepper, zucchini, jalapeño, chili powder, and cumin; stir to coat. Cook, stirring occasionally, until vegetables have begun to soften, about 5 minutes. Stir in broth, beans, and tomatoes and their juices; bring to a simmer and cook for 10 minutes. Add chicken and remaining 1/8 teaspoon salt. Return to a simmer and cook until chicken is cooked through, 5 to 7 minutes. Divide chili among 4 bowls, top with avocado, and serve.

CHAPTER 6
BURGERS, DOGS & OTHER MEAT DISHES

CHIMICHURRI BURGERS

 Prep: 15 min

 Cooking: 15 min

Serve: 4

NUTRITION:
Per serving with bun: 450 calories, 21 g fat, 7 g saturated fat, 40 g protein, 25 g carbohydrate, 4 g fiber, 490 mg sodium

INGREDIENTS

Sauce
- 1 cup parsley leaves
- 3 scallions, chopped
- 2 garlic cloves, chopped
- 2 tablespoons red wine vinegar
- 2 tablespoons water
- 1 tablespoon extra-virgin olive oil
- 1/2 teaspoon red pepper flakes
- 1/8 teaspoon salt

Burgers
- 1+1/2 pounds extra-lean ground beef
- 2 teaspoons dried basil
- 1/4 teaspoon freshly ground black pepper
- 1/8 teaspoon salt
- 4 whole-wheat or whole-grain hamburger buns, lightly toasted (optional)

DIRECTION

1. For the sauce: In a blender or food processor, combine parsley, scallions, garlic, vinegar, water, oil, pepper flakes, and salt; pulse until just puréed, about 1 minute. For the burgers: In a large bowl, combine beef, basil, black pepper, and salt. Form into 4 patties, about 1 inch thick. Lightly coat a grill or grill pan with cooking spray and heat to medium-high.
2. Grill burgers 5 to 6 minutes per side, or until a thermometer inserted into the thickest part registers 160°F. Serve burgers on buns, if using, topped with chimichurri sauce.

BEEF SATAY WITH PEANUT SAUCE

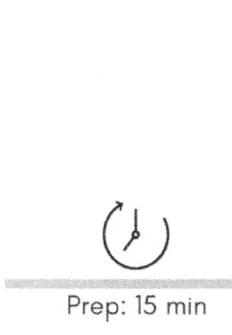
Prep: 15 min

Cooking: 15 min

Serve: 4

NUTRITION:
Per serving: 360 calories, 17 g fat, 4 g saturated fat, 43 g protein, 6 g carbohydrate, 1 g fiber, 460 mg sodium

INGREDIENTS

Satay
- 3 garlic cloves, minced
- 2 tablespoons fresh lime juice
- 1 tablespoon grated fresh ginger
- 1/2 teaspoon toasted sesame oil
- 1+1/2 pounds top round beef, trimmed and cut into 3/4-inchthick slices

Sauce
- 1/4 cup creamy trans-fat-free peanut butter
- 1/4 cup water
- 2 tablespoons low-sodium soy sauce
- 1 tablespoon plus 1+1/2 teaspoons rice vinegar
- 2 garlic cloves, minced
- 1/8 teaspoon red pepper flakes
- Special equipment
- 4 (12-inch) skewers

DIRECTION

1. For the satay: In a 9- by 13-inch glass baking dish, combine garlic, lime juice, ginger, and sesame oil. Add beef and turn to coat with marinade. Cover the dish with plastic wrap and marinate beef at room temperature for 20 minutes.
2. For the sauce: In a medium bowl, whisk together peanut butter, water, soy sauce, vinegar, garlic, and pepper flakes. Lightly coat a grill or grill pan with cooking spray and heat to medium-high. Thread equal amounts of sliced meat onto 4 skewers.
3. Grill meat 5 to 7 minutes per side for medium-rare. Serve warm with peanut sauce drizzled evenly over the meat or on the side for dipping.

GRILLED PORK TENDERLOIN WITH PEACH-LIME SALSA

Prep: 15 min

Cooking: 30 min

Serve: 4

NUTRITION:
Per serving with salsa: 270 calories, 8 g fat, 2.5 g saturated fat, 37 g protein, 12 g carbohydrate, 2 g fiber, 230 mg sodium

INGREDIENTS

- 2 garlic cloves, minced
- 2 teaspoons extra-virgin olive oil
- 1/4 teaspoon freshly ground black pepper
- 1+1/2 pounds pork tenderloin
- 2 large peaches, peeled and cut into 1/2-inch pieces
- 1 small red onion, minced
- 1/4 cup finely chopped fresh mint
- 3 tablespoons fresh lime juice
- 1/4 teaspoon salt

DIRECTION

1. In a small bowl, combine garlic, oil, and pepper to form a rough paste. Place pork in a 9- by 13-inch glass baking dish and coat with garlic paste; let stand at room temperature for 10 minutes.
2. While pork is standing, in another small bowl combine peaches, onion, mint, lime juice, and salt. Lightly coat a grill or grill pan with cooking spray and heat to medium-high.
3. Grill pork 12 to 14 minutes per side, or until a thermometer inserted into the thickest part reads 150°F to 155°F. Transfer pork to a cutting board and let rest for 5 to 10 minutes. Slice pork into 1/2-inch-thick slices and serve warm with peach-lime salsa.

CHIPOTLE CHILI DOGS

Prep: 15 min

Cooking: 20 min

Serve: 4

NUTRITION:
Per serving with bun: 340 calories, 15 g fat, 6 g saturated fat, 23 g protein, 29 g carbohydrate, 4 g fiber, 920 mg sodium

INGREDIENTS

- 1 teaspoon extra-virgin olive oil
- 1 small onion, finely chopped
- 2 garlic cloves, minced
- 1/2 pound extra-lean ground beef
- 2 tablespoons tomato paste
- 1 canned chipotle chile in adobo, chopped, plus 1 teaspoon sauce from can
- 3/4 cup lower-sodium beef broth
- 4 reduced-fat beef hot dogs
- 4 whole-wheat or whole-grain hot dog buns, lightly toasted (optional)

DIRECTION

1. In a medium saucepan, heat oil over medium heat. Add onion and garlic; cook, stirring occasionally, until translucent, 4 to 5 minutes. Add beef, increase the heat to high, and cook, breaking up meat with a spoon and stirring just until all pink is gone, 2 to 3 minutes more. Reduce the heat to medium and stir in tomato paste, chile, and adobo sauce. Add broth and bring to a simmer. Reduce the heat to low, cover, and cook until meat is cooked through, about 5 minutes.
2. While chili is cooking, lightly coat a grill or grill pan with cooking spray and heat to medium-high. Grill hot dogs, turning occasionally, until lightly browned and heated through, 5 to 7 minutes. Serve hot dogs on buns, if using, topped with chili

HERB-MARINATED SIRLOIN WITH ROASTED ASPARAGUS AND TOMATOES

 Prep: 10 min

 Cooking: 30 min

 Serve: 4

NUTRITION:
Per serving: 280 calories, 10 g fat, 3.5 g saturated fat, 40 g protein, 7 g carbohydrate, 3 g fiber, 250 mg sodium

INGREDIENTS

- 1/2 teaspoon garlic powder
- 1/2 teaspoon dried marjoram
- 1/2 teaspoon dried thyme
- 1/2 teaspoon freshly ground black pepper
- 1/4 teaspoon salt
- 1 (1+3/4-pound) sirloin steak, about 1+1/2 inches thick
- 1 pound medium-thick asparagus, trimmed
- 1+1/2 cups grape tomatoes
- 2 teaspoons extra-virgin olive oil

DIRECTION

1. In a small bowl, combine garlic powder, marjoram, thyme, pepper, and 1/8 teaspoon of the salt. Rub onto steak. Place steak on a plate, cover with plastic wrap, and let steak sit at room temperature for 30 minutes.
2. Lightly coat a heavy skillet with cooking spray and heat over medium-high heat. Pan-grill steak 10 minutes per side for medium-rare. Transfer to a cutting board and let sit for 5 to 10 minutes.
3. While steak is resting, heat the oven to 450°F. Spread asparagus and tomatoes on a baking sheet, drizzle with oil, sprinkle with remaining 1/8 teaspoon salt, and toss to combine. Roast until tomatoes are bursting and asparagus is tender, 8 to 10 minutes.
4. While vegetables are roasting, thinly slice steak. Divide steak and vegetables among 4 plates and serve warm.

CARNE ASADA

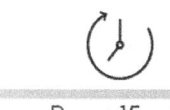
Prep: 15 min

Cooking: 30 min

Serve: 4

NUTRITION:
Per serving: 360 calories, 17 g fat, 5 g saturated fat, 38 g protein, 13 g carbohydrate, 3 g fiber, 440 mg sodium

INGREDIENTS

- 1/4 cup fresh lime juice
- 2 garlic cloves, minced
- 1/2 teaspoon freshly ground black pepper
- 1/8 teaspoon salt
- 1 (1+1/2-pound) flank steak, about 1 inch thick
- 1 large red onion, sliced into 1/4-inch-thick rounds
- 1/2 teaspoon extra-virgin olive oil
- 1 small avocado, sliced into 1/4-inch-thick pieces
- 1 cup fresh tomato salsa

DIRECTION

1. In a 9- by 13-inch glass baking dish, combine lime juice, garlic, pepper, and salt. Add steak and turn to coat.
2. Cover the dish with plastic wrap and marinate steak at room temperature for 20 minutes, turning once. Lightly coat a grill or grill pan with cooking spray and heat to medium-high.
3. Grill steak, basting with any remaining marinade, 5 to 7 minutes per side for medium-rare. Transfer to a cutting board and let rest for 5 to 10 minutes. While steak is resting, in a medium bowl toss onion with oil.
4. Grill, turning occasionally, until golden, 4 to 5 minutes. Cut steak into thin slices across the grain and divide among 4 plates. Serve with onion, avocado, and salsa.

KOFTA SKEWERS WITH PEPPERS

Prep: 20 min   Cooking: 17 min

Serve: 4

NUTRITION:
Per serving: 360 calories, 21 g fat, 9 g saturated fat, 35 g protein, 8 g carbohydrate, 2 g fiber, 330 mg sodium

INGREDIENTS

- 1 pound extra-lean ground beef
- 1/2 pound lean ground lamb
- 1 small onion, grated
- 1/4 cup chopped fresh parsley
- 2 tablespoons tomato paste
- 2 garlic cloves, minced
- 1 tablespoon ground cumin
- 1 teaspoon red pepper flakes
- 1/4 teaspoon salt
- 2 medium bell peppers, any color, cut into 1/2-inch-wide strips
- 1 teaspoon extra-virgin olive oil
- Special equipment
- 8 (12-inch) skewers

DIRECTION

1. In a large bowl, combine beef, lamb, onion, parsley, tomato paste, garlic, cumin, pepper flakes, and salt.
2. Divide meat mixture into 8 equal portions. Form each portion into a 6-inch sausage shape around a skewer. In a medium bowl, toss peppers with oil. Lightly coat a grill or grill pan with cooking spray and heat to medium-high.
3. Grill meat, turning frequently, until browned on all sides and cooked through, about 15 minutes. Halfway through cooking, place peppers on the grill and cook, turning frequently, until lightly charred on all sides, 8 to 10 minutes. Serve kofta hot with peppers.

PORK KEBABS WITH SCALLION-CHILI PASTE

Prep: 15 min Cooking: 15 min Serve: 4

NUTRITION:
Per serving: 240 calories, 5 g fat, 1.5 g saturated fat, 40 g protein, 6 g carbohydrate, 2 g fiber, 560 mg sodium

INGREDIENTS

- 6 scallions, roughly chopped
- 1/2 cup cilantro leaves
- 1 tablespoon rice vinegar
- 2 teaspoons Asian fish sauce
- 1 teaspoon chili paste (from a jar)
- 1+1/2 pounds pork top loin, cut into 1-inch cubes
- 2 medium zucchini, cut into 1-inch-thick rounds
- 2 garlic cloves, minced
- 1 teaspoon canola oil
- Salt and freshly ground black pepper

Special equipment
- 8 (12-inch) skewers

DIRECTION

1. In a food processor, combine scallions and cilantro; pulse until finely chopped. Add vinegar, fish sauce, and chili paste; process until a rough paste forms, about 30 seconds.
2. Transfer scallion-chili paste to a medium bowl, add pork, and turn to coat well. In another medium bowl, toss zucchini with garlic and oil. Thread pork and zucchini evenly onto skewers, alternating pieces.
3. Lightly coat a grill or grill pan with cooking spray and heat to medium-high. Grill kebabs, turning frequently, until pork is just cooked through, 10 to 12 minutes. Season lightly with salt and pepper and serve.

HOT DOGS WITH HOMEMADE TOMATO-PICKLE RELISH

 Prep: 15 min   Cooking: 10 min

 Serve: 4

NUTRITION:
Per serving with bun: 230 calories, 9 g fat, 3.5 g saturated fat, 10 g protein, 28 g carbohydrate, 4 g fiber, 850 mg sodium

INGREDIENTS

- 3/4 cup finely chopped bell pepper (mix of green and yellow)
- 1 medium plum tomato, finely chopped
- 1/4 cup finely chopped red onion
- 2 tablespoons finely chopped dill pickle
- 1 tablespoon cider vinegar
- 1/4 teaspoon granular sugar substitute
- 1/8 teaspoon salt
- 4 reduced-fat beef hot dogs
- 4 whole-wheat or whole-grain hot dog buns, lightly toasted (optional)

DIRECTION

1. In a small bowl, combine pepper, tomato, onion, pickle, vinegar, sugar substitute, and salt.
2. Lightly coat a grill or grill pan with cooking spray and heat to medium-high. Grill hot dogs, turning occasionally, until lightly browned and heated through, 5 to 7 minutes. Serve hot dogs on buns, if using, topped with relish.

PORK PINCHOS WITH SHREDDED CABBAGE SALAD

Prep: 30 min

Cooking: 15 min

Serve: 4

NUTRITION:
Per serving: 390 calories, 20 g fat, 5 g saturated fat, 40 g protein, 13 g carbohydrate, 5 g fiber, 240 mg sodium

INGREDIENTS

Pork
- 2 teaspoons paprika
- 1 teaspoon ground cumin
- 1/2 teaspoon garlic powder
- 1/4 teaspoon cayenne
- 1+1/2 pounds pork center loin, cut into 1-inch cubes

Salad
- 1 (1 pound) head Napa cabbage, thinly sliced (6 cups)
- 1 seedless orange, peeled and chopped
- 1 small avocado, finely chopped
- 2 scallions, thinly sliced
- 1 tablespoon extra-virgin olive oil
- 1/4 teaspoon salt
- 1/4 teaspoon freshly ground black pepper
- Pinch cayenne
- 1 small orange, peeled and cut into 8 wedges
- **Special equipment**
- 4 (12-inch) skewers

DIRECTION

1. For the pork: In a large bowl, combine paprika, cumin, garlic powder, and cayenne. Add pork and turn to coat; cover the bowl with plastic wrap and let sit at room temperature for 30 minutes. Thread pork evenly onto skewers.
2. For the salad: In another large bowl, combine cabbage, chopped orange, avocado, scallions, oil, salt, black pepper, and cayenne. Transfer salad to a large platter.
3. Lightly coat a grill or grill pan with cooking spray and heat to medium-high. Grill pork, turning frequently, until cooked through, 10 to 12 minutes.
4. Serve warm on top of salad, and put orange wedges on the side.

MIDDLE EASTERN STEAK AND CHICKPEA SALAD

Prep: 15 min

Cooking: 10 min

Serve: 4

NUTRITION:
Per serving: 360 calories, 14 g fat, 5 g saturated fat, 33 g protein, 25 g carbohydrate, 5 g fiber, 660 mg sodium

INGREDIENTS

- 1 pound flank steak
- 1 (15.5-ounce) can chickpeas, rinsed and drained
- 4 ounces baby spinach (4 cups)
- 1 large cucumber, finely chopped
- 2 ounces reduced-fat feta cheese, crumbled (1/3 cup)
- 4 pepperoncini (from a jar)
- 1/2 cup parsley leaves
- 1/4 cup roughly chopped fresh mint
- 1 garlic clove, minced
- 1 tablespoon fresh lemon juice
- 2 teaspoons extra-virgin olive oil

DIRECTION

1. Lightly coat a grill or grill pan with cooking spray and heat to medium-high. Grill steak 4 minutes per side for medium-rare. Transfer to a cutting board and let rest for 5 to 10 minutes.
2. While steak is resting, in a large bowl combine chickpeas, spinach, cucumber, feta, pepperoncini, parsley, mint, garlic, lemon juice, and oil.
3. Slice steak thinly across the grain. Add steak and its juices to chickpea salad and toss. Serve warm or at room temperature.

GRILLED STEAK WITH TEXAS MOP SAUCE

 Prep: 10 min

 Cooking: 10 min

 Serve: 4

NUTRITION:
Per serving: 299 calories, 14 g fat, 5 g saturated fat, 37 g protein, 5 g carbohydrate, 0 g fiber, 180 mg sodium

INGREDIENTS

- 1/2 cup no-salt-added tomato sauce
- 1/4 cup strongly brewed decaffeinated coffee
- 2 tablespoons Worcestershire sauce
- 1 tablespoon sugar-free pancake syrup
- 1 (1+1/2-pound) sirloin steak, about 1+1/2 inches thick
- 1 teaspoon freshly ground black pepper

DIRECTION

1. In a small saucepan, combine tomato sauce, coffee, Worcestershire sauce, and syrup. Bring to a simmer and remove from the heat. Transfer 1/3 cup of the sauce to a small bowl and reserve for dipping.
2. Lightly coat a grill or grill pan with cooking spray and heat to medium-high. Rub steak on both sides with pepper. Grill steak, basting frequently with remaining 1/3 cup mop sauce, 5 to 7 minutes per side for medium-rare. Allow steak to rest for 5 to 10 minutes.
3. Cut steak into thin slices, divide evenly among 4 plates, and serve with reserved mop sauce for dipping.

FETA-STUFFED SIRLOIN BURGERS WITH SUN-DRIED TOMATO MAYONNAISE

 Prep: 15 min

 Cooking: 10 min

 Serve: 4

NUTRITION:
Per serving with bun: 410 calories, 19 g fat, 7 g saturated fat, 35 g protein, 26 g carbohydrate, 4 g fiber, 718 mg sodium

INGREDIENTS

Mayonnaise
- 1/4 cup reduced-fat sour cream
- 8 sun-dried tomatoes in oil, drained and chopped
- 2 tablespoons mayonnaise

Burgers
- 1 pound ground sirloin
- 4 ounces reduced-fat feta cheese, crumbled (1/3 cup)
- 1 teaspoon dried oregano
- 1/4 teaspoon red pepper flakes
- 4 whole-wheat or whole-grain hamburger buns, lightly toasted (optional)
- 1 small cucumber, thinly sliced

DIRECTION

1. For the mayonnaise: In a small bowl, combine sour cream, tomatoes, and mayonnaise.
2. For the burgers: In a large bowl, combine sirloin, cheese, oregano, and pepper flakes. Form mixture into 4 patties, about 1/2 inch thick.
3. Lightly coat a large nonstick skillet with cooking spray and heat over medium-high heat. Cook burgers until browned on both sides, 3 to 4 minutes per side, or until a thermometer inserted into the thickest part registers 160°F.
4. Serve burgers on buns, if using, and top with mayonnaise and cucumber.

MOROCCAN SPICE-RUBBED PORK CHOPS

Prep: 10 min Cooking: 20 min Serve: 4

NUTRITION:
Per serving: 230 calories, 10 g fat, 3 g saturated fat, 32 g protein, 1 g carbohydrate, 0 g fiber, 210 mg sodium

INGREDIENTS

- 2 garlic cloves, minced
- 1 teaspoon extra-virgin olive oil
- 1/2 teaspoon ground cinnamon
- 1/2 teaspoon ground coriander
- 1/2 teaspoon ground cumin
- 1/2 teaspoon paprika
- 4 (6-ounce) center rib pork chops, about 1/2 inch thick
- 1/4 teaspoon salt
- Freshly ground black pepper
- 4 lemon wedges

DIRECTION

1. In a small bowl, combine garlic, oil, cinnamon, coriander, cumin, and paprika to form a rough paste. Press spice mixture onto both sides of each pork chop.
2. Lightly coat a grill or grill pan with cooking spray and heat to medium-high. Grill pork until there is no trace of pink near the bone, 6 to 8 minutes per side. Sprinkle with salt and season with pepper to taste. Divide among 4 plates and serve hot with lemon wedges.

GRILLED PORK AND PLUM SALAD WITH ALMOND GREMOLATA

 Prep: 10 min   Cooking: 20 min

 Serve: 4

NUTRITION:
Per serving: 340 calories, 14 g fat, 3 g saturated fat, 39 g protein, 17 g carbohydrate, 4 g fiber, 290 mg sodium

INGREDIENTS

Gremolata
- 1/4 cup slivered almonds
- 1 garlic clove, peeled
- 1/2 cup parsley leaves
- 1 teaspoon finely grated lemon zest
- 1 teaspoon extra-virgin olive oil
- 1/8 teaspoon salt

Pork
- 2 (3.4-pound) pork tenderloins
- 4 firm medium plums, halved
- 1 tablespoon extra-virgin olive oil
- 2 teaspoons red wine vinegar
- 1 teaspoon finely grated lemon zest
- 1/8 teaspoon salt
- 1/8 teaspoon freshly ground black pepper
- 6 ounces baby spinach (6 cups)

DIRECTION

1. For the gremolata: In a food processor, combine almonds and garlic; pulse just until blended, about 10 seconds. Add parsley, lemon zest, oil, and salt; pulse just until blended, about 15 seconds more. For the pork: Lightly coat a grill or grill pan with cooking spray and heat to medium-high.
2. Grill pork 8 to 10 minutes per side, or until a thermometer inserted into the thickest part reads 150°F to 155°F.
3. During the last 5 minutes of cooking, place plums, skin side down, on grill and cook, turning once. Transfer pork and plums to a cutting board and let pork rest for 5 to 10 minutes. While pork is resting, slice plums into wedges. In a large bowl, combine oil, vinegar, lemon zest, salt, and pepper.
4. Add plums and spinach and toss to combine. Cut pork into 1/2-inch-thick slices. Divide pork among 4 plates and top with gremolata. Serve warm with salad.

SPICY LAMB KEBABS WITH CUCUMBER-MINT YOGURT

Prep: 20 min

Cooking: 15 min

Serve: 4

NUTRITION:
Per serving: 301 calories, 11 g fat, 4 g saturated fat, 40 g protein, 10 g carbohydrate, 1 g fiber, 420 mg sodium

INGREDIENTS

- 1 teaspoon ground cumin
- 1/2 teaspoon ground coriander
- 1/2 teaspoon freshly ground black pepper
- 1/4 teaspoon cayenne
- 1+1/2 pounds leg of lamb, cut into 24 (1+1/2-inch) cubes
- 4 tablespoons fresh lemon juice
- 1 teaspoon extra-virgin olive oil
- 1 cup nonfat or low-fat Greek-style plain yogurt
- 1 small cucumber, peeled, seeded, and finely chopped
- 2 tablespoons finely chopped fresh mint
- 2 garlic cloves, minced
- 1/2 teaspoon salt
- 2 medium red onions, cut into 16 wedges

Special equipment
- 8 (12-inch) skewers

DIRECTION

1. In a large bowl, combine cumin, coriander, 1/4 teaspoon of the black pepper, and cayenne. Add lamb and toss to coat. Add 3 tablespoons of the lemon juice and oil; toss again. Cover the bowl with plastic wrap and marinate lamb at room temperature for 20 minutes
2. While lamb is marinating, in a medium bowl combine yogurt, cucumber, mint, garlic, salt, remaining 1 tablespoon lemon juice, and remaining 1/4 teaspoon black pepper.
3. Lightly coat a grill or grill pan with cooking spray and heat to medium-high. Thread 3 lamb cubes and 2 onion wedges onto each skewer, alternating pieces. Grill kebabs, turning frequently, 5 to 7 minutes for medium-rare. Divide among 4 plates and serve warm with cucumber-mint yogurt.

CHAPTER 7
VEGETARIAN'S PARADISE

SEARED TEMPEH AND THREE-BEAN SALAD

Prep: 15 min   Cooking: 20 min   Serve: 4

NUTRITION:

Per serving: 340 calories, 6 g fat, 1.5 g saturated fat, 19 g protein, 53 g carbohydrate, 15 g fiber, 440 mg sodium

INGREDIENTS

- 2 tablespoons fresh lemon juice
- 1 tablespoon extra-virgin olive oil
- 3 teaspoons low-sodium soy sauce
- 2 teaspoons Dijon mustard
- 2 garlic cloves, minced
- 1/8 teaspoon freshly ground black pepper
- 1/8 teaspoon granular sugar substitute
- 1 (15-ounce) can kidney beans, rinsed and drained
- 1 (15-ounce) can white beans, rinsed and drained
- 12 ounces green beans, trimmed and cut into 1-inch pieces
- 1 (8-ounce) package three-grain or regular tempeh, cut into 1/4-inch cubes
- 4 scallions, thinly sliced
- 1/4 cup chopped fresh parsley
- 1 cup cherry tomatoes, halved

DIRECTION

1. In a large bowl, whisk together lemon juice, oil, 1 teaspoon of the soy sauce, mustard, garlic, pepper, and sugar substitute. Add kidney beans and white beans; stir to combine.
2. Bring a large saucepan of lightly salted water to a boil. Add green beans, return to a boil, and cook until crisp-tender, about 2 minutes. Drain in a colander and immediately run under very cold water to stop cooking. Drain again and pat dry. Add to the bowl with other beans and toss to combine.
3. Lightly coat a large nonstick skillet with cooking spray and heat over medium-high heat. Add tempeh and remaining 2 teaspoons soy sauce. Cook, turning occasionally, until tempeh is browned on all sides, 4 to 6 minutes. Transfer tempeh to the bowl with beans and add scallions and parsley; toss to combine.
4. Divide salad among 4 plates, top with tomatoes, and serve warm.

SPAGHETTI WITH RICOTTA AND FRESH TOMATO SAUCE

Prep: 15 min

Cooking: 20 min

Serve: 4

NUTRITION:

Per serving: 310 calories, 8 g fat, 3.5 g saturated fat, 16 g protein, 49 g carbohydrate, 8 g fiber, 300 mg sodium

INGREDIENTS

- 8 ounces whole-wheat spaghetti
- 6 large plum tomatoes, finely chopped
- 3/4 cup part-skim ricotta cheese
- 1/4 cup freshly grated Parmesan cheese
- 1/2 cup chopped fresh basil, plus basil leaves for garnish
- 3 garlic cloves, minced
- 2 teaspoons extra-virgin olive oil
- 1/4 teaspoon salt
- 1/8 teaspoon freshly ground black pepper

DIRECTION

1. Bring a large pot of lightly salted water to a boil. Add spaghetti and cook according to package directions until al dente.
2. While pasta is cooking, in a large bowl combine tomatoes, ricotta, Parmesan, chopped basil, and garlic.
3. Reserving 1/4 cup of the pasta cooking liquid, drain pasta. Add pasta to the bowl with tomato mixture. Add oil, salt, and pepper; toss gently. Add reserved cooking liquid and stir to make a sauce. Garnish with basil leaves and serve warm.

GRILLED TOMATO, ARUGULA, AND FETA CHEESE PIZZAS

Prep: 10 min

Cooking: 5 min

Serve: 4

NUTRITION:
Per serving: 190 calories, 8 g fat, 2.5 g saturated fat, 8 g protein, 22 g carbohydrate, 4 g fiber, 590 mg sodium

INGREDIENTS

- 4 (8-inch) whole-wheat tortillas
- 4 medium plum tomatoes, thinly sliced
- 3+1/2 ounces reduced-fat feta cheese, crumbled (generous 1/3 cup)
- 1 garlic clove, minced
- 2 tablespoons thinly sliced fresh basil
- 1+1/3 cups baby arugula
- 2 teaspoons extra-virgin olive oil
- Salt and freshly ground black pepper

DIRECTION

1. Lightly coat a grill or grill pan with cooking spray and heat to medium-high.
2. Grill tortillas until lightly puffed and browned on the bottom, about 1 minute. Transfer to a cutting board, grilled side up, and top tortillas evenly with tomatoes, cheese, garlic, and basil.
3. Return tortillas to the grill, topping side up. Cover and cook until cheese is softened, about 30 seconds. Top with arugula, cover, and grill another 1 to 2 minutes, or until arugula is wilted. Transfer pizzas to 4 plates, drizzle with oil, and season with salt and pepper. Serve warm.

GRILLED SPINACH, GARLIC, AND GOAT CHEESE PIZZAS

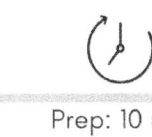
Prep: 10 min

Cooking: 5 min

Serve: 4

NUTRITION:
Per serving: 180 calories, 6 g fat, 2 g saturated fat, 6 g protein, 27 g carbohydrate, 6 g fiber, 580 mg sodium

INGREDIENTS

- 1/2 teaspoon extra-virgin olive oil
- 6 ounces baby spinach (6 cups)
- 3 garlic cloves, minced
- 1 tablespoon water
- 4 (8-inch) whole-wheat tortillas
- 4 medium plum tomatoes, thinly sliced
- 4 ounces reduced-fat goat cheese, crumbled (2/3 cup)
- 1/4 teaspoon salt
- Freshly ground black pepper

DIRECTION

1. In a large nonstick skillet, heat oil over medium heat. Add spinach and garlic; cook, stirring, about 30 seconds. Add water, cover, and reduce the heat to low. Cook until spinach is wilted, 1 to 2 minutes more.
2. Lightly coat a grill or grill pan with cooking spray and heat to medium-high. Grill tortillas until lightly puffed and browned on the bottom, about 1 minute. Transfer to a cutting board, grilled side up, and top tortillas evenly with tomatoes, spinach, and cheese. Return tortillas to the grill, topping side up.
3. Cover and cook until cheese is melted, about 1 minute. Transfer pizzas to 4 plates, sprinkle with salt, and season with pepper to taste. Serve warm.

GRILLED SPINACH, GARLIC, AND GOAT CHEESE PIZZAS

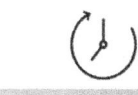
Prep: 10 min

Cooking: 5 min

Serve: 4

NUTRITION:
Per serving: 180 calories, 6 g fat, 2 g saturated fat, 6 g protein, 27 g carbohydrate, 6 g fiber, 580 mg sodium

INGREDIENTS

- 1/2 teaspoon extra-virgin olive oil
- 6 ounces baby spinach (6 cups)
- 3 garlic cloves, minced
- 1 tablespoon water
- 4 (8-inch) whole-wheat tortillas
- 4 medium plum tomatoes, thinly sliced
- 4 ounces reduced-fat goat cheese, crumbled (2/3 cup)
- 1/4 teaspoon salt
- Freshly ground black pepper

DIRECTION

1. In a large nonstick skillet, heat oil over medium heat. Add spinach and garlic; cook, stirring, about 30 seconds. Add water, cover, and reduce the heat to low. Cook until spinach is wilted, 1 to 2 minutes more.
2. Lightly coat a grill or grill pan with cooking spray and heat to medium-high. Grill tortillas until lightly puffed and browned on the bottom, about 1 minute. Transfer to a cutting board, grilled side up, and top tortillas evenly with tomatoes, spinach, and cheese. Return tortillas to the grill, topping side up.
3. Cover and cook until cheese is melted, about 1 minute. Transfer pizzas to 4 plates, sprinkle with salt, and season with pepper to taste. Serve warm.

GRILLED ROASTED PEPPER, RED ONION, AND MOZZARELLA PIZZAS

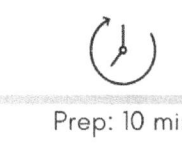
Prep: 10 min

Cooking: 5 min

Serve: 4

NUTRITION:
Per serving: 180 calories, 6 g fat, 2 g saturated fat, 6 g protein, 27 g carbohydrate, 6 g fiber, 580 mg sodium

INGREDIENTS

- 1/2 teaspoon extra-virgin olive oil
- 6 ounces baby spinach (6 cups)
- 3 garlic cloves, minced
- 1 tablespoon water
- 4 (8-inch) whole-wheat tortillas
- 4 medium plum tomatoes, thinly sliced
- 4 ounces reduced-fat goat cheese, crumbled (2/3 cup)
- 1/4 teaspoon salt
- Freshly ground black pepper

DIRECTION

1. In a large nonstick skillet, heat oil over medium heat. Add spinach and garlic; cook, stirring, about 30 seconds. Add water, cover, and reduce the heat to low. Cook until spinach is wilted, 1 to 2 minutes more.
2. Lightly coat a grill or grill pan with cooking spray and heat to medium-high. Grill tortillas until lightly puffed and browned on the bottom, about 1 minute. Transfer to a cutting board, grilled side up, and top tortillas evenly with tomatoes, spinach, and cheese. Return tortillas to the grill, topping side up.
3. Cover and cook until cheese is melted, about 1 minute. Transfer pizzas to 4 plates, sprinkle with salt, and season with pepper to taste. Serve warm.

ASIAN MARINATED TOFU AND EGGPLANT WITH RICE

Prep: 15 min

Cooking: 20 min

Serve: 4

NUTRITION:
Per serving: 240 calories, 12 g fat, 2 g saturated fat, 14 g protein, 21 g carbohydrate, 4 g fiber, 290 mg sodium

INGREDIENTS

- 3 tablespoons rice vinegar
- 4 garlic cloves, minced
- 1 tablespoon grated fresh ginger
- 1 tablespoon low-sodium soy sauce
- 1 teaspoon toasted sesame oil
- 1 (14-ounce) package extra-firm tofu, cut into 1-inch cubes
- 1 cup quick-cooking whole-grain brown rice
- 1 tablespoon extra-virgin olive oil
- 12 ounces Japanese or baby eggplants, cut into 1/2-inch cubes
- 1/4 teaspoon salt
- 4 ounces snow peas, trimmed
- 1/4 cup water

DIRECTION

1. In a 9- by 13-inch glass baking dish, stir together vinegar, 2 teaspoons of the garlic, ginger, soy sauce, and sesame oil. Lay tofu cubes between paper towels and press to remove excess moisture. Add tofu to the baking dish with marinade and turn gently to coat well. Cover the dish with plastic wrap and marinate tofu for 20 minutes at room temperature.
2. While tofu is marinating, cook rice according to package directions. Remove from the heat and keep warm. While rice is cooking, in a large nonstick skillet heat oil over medium-high heat. Add remaining garlic and cook for 1 minute. Add eggplant and salt; cook, stirring, until eggplant is browned on all sides, 4 to 5 minutes. Transfer eggplant to a large bowl.
3. Add snow peas and water to the skillet, cover, and cook over medium-high heat until snow peas are crisp-tender, 2 to 3 minutes. Transfer snow peas to the bowl with eggplant.
4. Add tofu and marinade to the skillet and cook over medium-high heat, turning with a spatula occasionally, until tofu is browned and crisped on all sides, 6 to 8 minutes. Return vegetables to the skillet and cook, gently stirring to combine with tofu, just until heated through, about 1 minute. Divide rice among 4 plates and serve with tofu and vegetables.

INDIAN VEGETABLE CURRY

 Prep: 15 min

 Cooking: 20 min

 Serve: 4

NUTRITION:

Per serving: 200 calories, 5 g fat, 1 g saturated fat, 9 g protein, 32 g carbohydrate, 7 g fiber, 490 mg sodium

INGREDIENTS

- 4 garlic cloves, peeled
- 1 (2-inch) piece fresh ginger
- 1 tablespoon extra-virgin olive oil
- 1 small red onion, finely chopped
- 1+1/2 teaspoons curry powder
- 3/4 teaspoon cumin seeds
- 1/8 teaspoon cayenne
- 1+1/4 cups canned diced tomatoes
- 1 cup low-fat or nonfat plain yogurt
- 1/4 teaspoon salt
- 1+1/2 cups small cauliflower florets
- 4 ounces green beans, trimmed and cut into 1-inch pieces
- 1 cup canned chickpeas, rinsed and drained
- 1/3 cup water
- 1 medium zucchini, cut into 1/4-inch cubes
- 1/4 cup finely chopped fresh cilantro

DIRECTION

1. In a food processor, combine garlic and ginger; pulse until finely chopped.
2. In a medium saucepan, heat oil over medium-high heat.
3. Add garlic mixture, onion, curry powder, cumin seeds, and cayenne; stir well. Reduce the heat to medium-low and cook, stirring frequently, until onion is softened, about 5 minutes. Add tomatoes, 3/4 cup of the yogurt, and salt; stir to combine. Add cauliflower, bring to a gentle simmer, and cook for 10 minutes.
4. Add green beans, chickpeas, and water; cover and simmer for 10 minutes more. Add zucchini and continue to cook, covered, until vegetables are tender, about 8 minutes more.
5. Spoon curry into 4 bowls and season lightly with additional salt, if desired. Top with remaining yogurt and sprinkle with cilantro. Serve warm

CHICAGO-STYLE GRILLED TOFU DOGS

Prep: 10 min

Cooking: 7 min

Serve: 4

NUTRITION:
Per serving with bun: 200 calories, 5 g fat, 1.5 g saturated fat, 12 g protein, 57 g carbohydrate, 4 g fiber, 680 mg sodium

INGREDIENTS

- 4 low-fat tofu hot dogs
- 4 whole-wheat or whole-grain hot dog buns, lightly toasted (optional)
- 4 teaspoons yellow mustard
- 1 large plum tomato, halved and thinly sliced
- 1/4 cup no-sugar-added pickle relish
- 4 pepperoncini (from a jar), thinly sliced
- 2 tablespoons minced white onion
- 1/4 teaspoon celery salt (optional)

DIRECTION

1. Lightly coat a grill or grill pan with cooking spray and heat to medium-high.
2. Grill hot dogs, turning frequently, until well browned on all sides, 3 to 5 minutes. Transfer hot dogs to buns, if using.
3. Top each hot dog with equal portions of mustard, tomato, relish, pepperoncini, and onion. Season with celery salt, if using. Serve warm.

SPICY SOUTH BEACH DIET MACARONI AND CHEESE

Prep: 10 min
Cooking: 35 min
Serve: 4

NUTRITION:
Per serving: 360 calories, 12 g fat, 6 g saturated fat, 18 g protein, 51 g carbohydrate, 6 g fiber, 280 mg sodium

INGREDIENTS

- 8 ounces whole-wheat or spelt elbow pasta
- 1 tablespoon trans-fat-free margarine
- 1 tablespoon whole-wheat flour
- 1/4 teaspoon cayenne
- 1+1/4 cups fat-free half-and-half
- 1 cup shredded reduced-fat sharp cheddar cheese
- 1/4 cup chopped fresh basil
- 1/4 teaspoon salt
- 2 large plum tomatoes, chopped
- Freshly ground black pepper

DIRECTION

1. Heat the oven to 400°F.
2. Bring a large saucepan of lightly salted water to a boil. Cook pasta according to package directions until al dente. Drain and rinse under cold water for 30 seconds.
3. While pasta is cooking, in a large nonstick skillet melt margarine over medium heat. Add flour and cayenne, reduce the heat to low, and whisk constantly until flour is incorporated, about 2 minutes.
4. Add half-and-half to the skillet, bring to a simmer over low heat, and cook, whisking frequently, until blended and thickened, 3 to 5 minutes. Add cheese, basil, and salt; stir until blended. Add pasta and stir until coated and warmed, about 1 minute; remove from the heat.
5. Lightly coat an 8- by 8-inch baking dish with cooking spray. Transfer macaroni and cheese to the baking dish. Sprinkle tomatoes on top and season with pepper. Bake until hot and bubbly, about 10 minutes. Place under the broiler and broil until the top is lightly browned, 3 to 4 minutes. Serve hot

TOFU SALAD SANDWICHES WITH TAPENADE

Prep: 15 min

Cooking: 10 min

Serve: 4

NUTRITION:
Per serving with bread: 239 calories, 10 g fat, 1.5 g saturated fat, 15 g protein, 22 g carbohydrate, 4 g fiber, 445 mg sodium

INGREDIENTS

- 1 teaspoon dried oregano
- 1 teaspoon garlic powder
- 1/4 teaspoon red pepper flakes
- 1 (14-ounce) package extra-firm tofu, cut into 1-inch cubes
- 2 large roasted red peppers (from a jar), drained, rinsed, and roughly chopped
- 12 basil leaves, roughly chopped
- 2 tablespoons olive tapenade (from a jar)
- 1 tablespoon mayonnaise
- 8 slices thin-sliced whole-grain bread, lightly toasted (optional)
- 2 cups baby arugula

DIRECTION

1. In a medium bowl, combine oregano, garlic powder, and pepper flakes. Place tofu cubes between paper towels and press to remove excess moisture. Transfer tofu to the bowl with oregano mixture and stir gently to coat well. Cover the bowl with plastic wrap and marinate tofu for 15 minutes at room temperature.
2. Lightly coat a large nonstick skillet with cooking spray and heat over medium-high heat. Add tofu, reduce the heat to medium, and cook, gently stirring, until tofu is golden brown on all sides, about 8 minutes. Remove from the heat and transfer tofu to the original medium bowl. Add peppers and basil; stir gently with a fork to break up tofu and combine
3. In a small bowl, stir together tapenade and mayonnaise. Spread tapenade mixture on 4 bread slices, if using, and top with tofu mixture, arugula, and remaining bread slices to form 4 sandwiches. Cut sandwiches in half and serve.

VIETNAMESE-STYLE VEGETABLES WITH RICE NOODLES

Prep: 20 min Cooking: 15 min Serve: 4

NUTRITION:

Per serving: 160 calories, 7 g fat, 1 g saturated fat, 4 g protein, 23 g carbohydrate, 4 g fiber, 480 mg sodium

INGREDIENTS

- 2 ounces rice noodles
- 1 tablespoon chili paste (from a jar)
- 1 tablespoon Asian fish sauce
- 1 tablespoon fresh lime juice
- 1 tablespoon rice vinegar
- 2 tablespoons extra-virgin olive oil
- 1 large head broccoli, cut into small florets (4 cups)
- 1 medium red bell pepper, thinly sliced
- 1 medium red onion, thinly sliced
- 1 medium zucchini, halved lengthwise and thinly sliced into half-moons
- 1/4 cup finely chopped fresh cilantro
- 4 lime wedges

DIRECTION

1. Place noodles in a medium bowl, cover with very warm tap water, and soak until softened, about 15 minutes. Drain and set aside.
2. While noodles are soaking, in a small bowl whisk together chili paste, fish sauce, lime juice, and vinegar.
3. In a large nonstick skillet, heat 1 tablespoon of the oil over medium-high heat. Add broccoli and toss to coat; cook, tossing gently, until tender, about 4 minutes. Transfer broccoli to a plate.
4. Add remaining 1 tablespoon oil to the skillet and heat over medium-high heat. Add pepper, onion, and zucchini; cook, stirring frequently, until vegetables are just beginning to soften, about 4 minutes. Return broccoli to the skillet and cook, stirring occasionally, for 3 minutes more. Stir in chili paste mixture, cover, and cook 1 minute more.
5. Add noodles to the skillet and toss well. Add cilantro and toss again. Divide among 4 plates and serve warm with lime wedges.

GRILLED TEMPEH BURGERS WITH HORSERADISH AIOLI

Prep: 25 min

Cooking: 10 min

Serve: 4

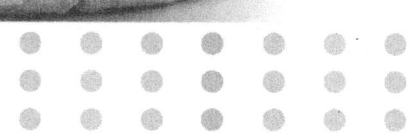

NUTRITION:
Per serving with bun: 330 calories, 13 g fat, 2.5 g saturated fat, 20 g protein, 32 g carbohydrate, 8 g fiber, 500 mg sodium

INGREDIENTS

Aioli
- 2 tablespoons mayonnaise
- 1+1/2 tablespoons prepared horseradish, drained well
- 1/2 teaspoon grated lemon zest
- 1 teaspoon fresh lemon juice
- 2 garlic cloves, minced

Burgers
- 4 scallions, roughly chopped
- 1/4 cup roughly chopped fresh parsley
- 1 garlic clove
- 1 (8-ounce) package tempeh, crumbled
- 2 teaspoons Dijon mustard
- 1 large egg
- 1/4 teaspoon salt
- 1/4 teaspoon freshly ground black pepper
- 4 whole-grain hamburger buns, lightly toasted (optional)
- 4 large Boston or red leaf lettuce leaves
- 1 large plum tomato, thinly sliced

DIRECTION

1. For the aioli: In a small bowl, stir together mayonnaise, horseradish, lemon zest, lemon juice, and garlic.
2. For the burgers: In a food processor, combine scallions, parsley, and garlic; process until finely chopped. Add tempeh, mustard, egg, salt, and pepper; pulse until mixture comes together. Form mixture into 4 patties, 1 inch thick. Lightly coat a grill or grill pan with cooking spray and heat to medium.
3. Grill burgers until browned and heated through, about 4 minutes per side. Place burgers on buns, if using, and top with aioli, lettuce, and tomato. Serve warm.

FARMERS' MARKET PASTA SALAD

Prep: 15 min Cooking: 25 min Serve: 4

NUTRITION:
Per serving: 340 calories, 6 g fat, 0.5 g saturated fat, 11 g protein, 65 g carbohydrate, 13 g fiber, 210 mg sodium

INGREDIENTS

- 8 ounces whole-wheat fusilli
- 1 tablespoon extra-virgin olive oil
- 1 medium red onion, finely chopped
- 1 large eggplant, cut into 3/4 -inch cubes
- 1/2 cup water
- 3 garlic cloves, minced
- 1 teaspoon dried thyme
- 1+1/2 cups grape tomatoes, halved
- 1/2 cup fresh or frozen corn kernels
- 1/2 cup fresh or frozen baby peas
- 1/2 cup chopped fresh basil
- 3 tablespoons red wine vinegar
- 1/4 teaspoon salt
- Freshly ground black pepper

DIRECTION

1. Bring a large saucepan of lightly salted water to a boil. Add pasta and cook according to package directions until al dente. Drain pasta and transfer to a large bowl.
2. While pasta is cooking, in a large nonstick skillet heat oil over medium-high heat. Add onion, reduce the heat to medium, and cook just until softened, about 5 minutes. Add eggplant, cover, and cook, stirring occasionally, until eggplant is softened, about 8 minutes. Add water, garlic, and thyme; stir to combine. Cook, uncovered, until the pan is almost dry, about 4 minutes. Add tomatoes, corn, and peas; cook until tomatoes begin to burst, about 5 minutes. Remove from the heat and stir in basil, vinegar, and salt; season to taste with pepper.
3. Add vegetables to pasta and toss well. Serve warm or at room temperature.

PEPPERY ZUCCHINI PASTA

Prep: 10 min

Cooking: 20 min

Serve: 4

NUTRITION:
Per serving: 280 calories, 5 g fat, 1.5 g saturated fat, 13 g protein, 46 g carbohydrate, 6 g fiber, 400 mg sodium

INGREDIENTS

- 2 teaspoons extra-virgin olive oil
- 1 small onion, finely chopped
- 3 garlic cloves, minced
- 3 pepperoncini (from a jar), minced
- 1/4 teaspoon salt
- 1/8 teaspoon freshly ground black pepper
- 8 ounces whole-wheat penne pasta
- 1 large zucchini, shredded
- 2 ounces reduced-fat goat cheese, crumbled (1/3 cup)
- 1 cup cherry or grape tomatoes, halved
- 1/4 cup chopped fresh basi

DIRECTION

1. In a large nonstick skillet, heat 1 teaspoon of the oil over medium-high heat. Add onion and garlic, reduce the heat to medium, and cook, stirring frequently, until onion is softened, 3 to 4 minutes. Add remaining 1 teaspoon oil, pepperoncini, salt, and pepper. Reduce the heat to low and continue cooking, stirring occasionally, for 2 to 3 minutes to flavor the oil. Remove from the heat and keep warm.
2. Bring a large pot of lightly salted water to a boil. Cook pasta according to package directions until al dente. Reserving 2 tablespoons of pasta cooking liquid, drain pasta.
3. Add pasta, reserved pasta cooking liquid, zucchini, cheese, tomatoes, and basil to skillet; toss to combine. Cook over medium heat until pasta is just heated through and cheese is melted, 1 to 2 minutes. Season with additional pepper to taste and serve warm.

BARBECUED TOFU WRAPS

 Prep: 15 min

 Cooking: 15 min

 Serve: 4

NUTRITION:
Per serving: 350 calories, 19 g fat, 2.5 g saturated fat, 16 g protein, 32 g carbohydrate, 9 g fiber, 390 mg sodium

INGREDIENTS

- 1 tablespoon extra-virgin olive oil
- 1 small onion, finely chopped
- 2 teaspoons garlic powder
- 2 teaspoons paprika
- 1 teaspoon mustard powder
- 1/2 teaspoon cayenne
- 2 tablespoons tomato paste
- 2 tablespoons Worcestershire
- 1 tablespoon granular sugar substitute
- 1/2 cup water
- 1 (14-ounce) package extra-firm tofu, cut into cubes
- 2 teaspoons fresh lime juice
- 4 (8-inch) whole-wheat tortillas
- 3 cups shredded romaine lettuce
- 1 small avocado, sliced

DIRECTION

1. In a medium skillet, heat oil over medium heat. Add onion, garlic powder, paprika, mustard, and cayenne; stir to combine. Cover and cook until onion is softened, about 5 minutes. Stir in tomato paste, Worcestershire sauce, and sugar substitute; cook, stirring, for 1 minute. Stir in water and cook 1 minute more. Add tofu, stir gently to coat with sauce, and cook until heated through, about 2 minutes. Remove from the heat, add lime juice, and stir to combine
2. Warm tortillas according to package directions. Place tortillas on a cutting board. Divide lettuce, avocado, and tofu among tortillas. Fold one side of each tortilla in and roll up tortillas to form wraps. Serve warm.

TEMPEH AND VEGETABLE FAJITAS

 Prep: 15 min   Cooking: 15 min

 Serve: 4

NUTRITION:
Per serving: 310 calories, 11 g fat, 2.5 g saturated fat, 16 g protein, 39 g carbohydrate, 9 g fiber, 740 mg sodium

INGREDIENTS
- 1/4 cup fresh lime juice
- 3 garlic cloves, minced
- 1 small serrano or jalapeno pepper, seeded and minced
- 3 teaspoons extra-virgin olive oil
- 2 teaspoons sugar-free pancake syrup
- 1 (8-ounce) package tempeh, cut crosswise into 3.4-inch strips
- 2 large bell peppers, any color, cut into wide strips
- 1 large red onion, cut into 1/4-inch-thick slices
- 1/4 teaspoon salt
- Freshly ground black pepper
- 4 (8-inch) whole-wheat tortillas
- 1 cup fresh salsa
- 1/4 cup reduced-fat sour cream

DIRECTION
1. In a 9- by 13-inch glass baking dish, whisk together lime juice, garlic, serrano pepper, 2 teaspoons of the oil, and syrup. Add tempeh, turn to coat, and arrange in a single layer. Cover the dish with plastic wrap and marinate the tempeh at room temperature for 30 minutes.
2. While tempeh is marinating, lightly coat a grill or grill pan with cooking spray and heat to medium-high. In a large bowl, toss bell peppers and onion with remaining 1 teaspoon oil, 1/8 teaspoon of the salt, and black pepper to taste. Grill vegetables until softened and browned, 8 to 10 minutes, turning halfway through. Transfer to a large platter.
3. Season tempeh with remaining 1/8 teaspoon salt and grill until lightly browned, 2 to 3 minutes per side. Transfer to the platter with the vegetables. Grill tortillas until lightly browned, about 1 minute per side.
4. Place 1 tortilla on each of 4 plates. Top with tempeh and grilled vegetables. Serve warm, topped with salsa and sour cream.

Made in the USA
Las Vegas, NV
24 June 2021